Red Hat Society®

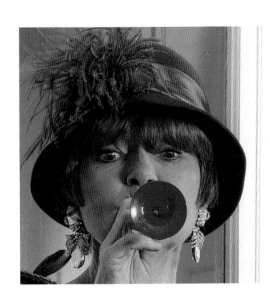

Red Hats

Red Hat Society

Red Hats

& the Women Who Wear Them

A LARK/CHAPELLE BOOK

A Division of Sterling Publishing Co., Inc.
New York

A Lark/Chapelle Book

Chapelle, Ltd., Inc.
P.O. Box 9255, Ogden, UT 84409
(801) 621-2777 • (801) 621-2788 Fax
e-mail: chapelle@chapelleltd.com
Web site: www.chapelleltd.com

Created and produced by Red Lips 4 Courage Communications, Inc.
www.redlips4courage.com
Eileen Cannon Paulin, President
Catherine Risling, Director of Editorial

10 9 8 7 6 5 4 3 2 1

First Edition

Published by Lark Books, A Division of
Sterling Publishing Co., Inc.
387 Park Avenue South, New York, N.Y. 10016

Distributed in Canada by Sterling Publishing, c/o Canadian Manda Group,
165 Dufferin Street, Toronto, Ontario, Canada M6K 3H6

Distributed in the United Kingdom by GMC Distribution Services,
Castle Place, 166 High Street, Lewes, East Sussex, England BN7 1XU

Distributed in Australia by Capricorn Link (Australia) Pty Ltd.,
P.O. Box 704, Windsor, NSW 2756 Australia

ISBN 13: 978-1-57990-994-9
ISBN 10: 1-57990-994-9

For information about custom editions, special sales, premium and corporate
purchases, please contact Sterling Special Sales Department at 800-805-5489
or specialsales@sterlingpub.com.

"A poet put it very well. She said when she was older,
She wouldn't be so meek and mild. She threatened to get bolder.
She'd put a red hat on her head and purple on her shoulder.
She'd make her life a warmer place, her golden years much golder."

—From "Ode to the Red Hat Society" by Sue Ellen Cooper

"The essence of design is having the imagination and the desire to create something." —Ruby RedHat

Foreword

Here I am (right), the newly anointed Exalted Queen Mother, at our very first Red Hat Society tea in April 1998. Vice Queen Linda Murphy is wearing the bowler I had given her as a gift, which sparked the beginning of our sisterhood. I am wearing my very first red hat—a fedora I purchased at a thrift store. I thought I could get by wearing lavender, but later realized my error and repented!

We women today pride ourselves on our ability to multi-task. We play so many roles in our lives—wife, mother, employee, homemaker, hobbyist, and caretaker. Doing many things successfully is not only an art; it is now considered a life requirement. In the course of an average day we are called on to shift mental gears again and again. Often, we refer to this process as "changing hats."

There are so many kinds of special hats. There are stocking caps, cocktail hats, beach hats, baseball caps, mouse ears, cowboy hats, hard hats, sailor's hats—ad infinitum.

This book is about *red* hats (and yes, pink ones as well). Why hats? Because, to the members of the Red Hat Society, as well as the public at large, our colorful hats have come to symbolize playtime and recess for the women who wear them. Anytime Red Hatters gather together—with other women in their chapter or in a large gathering of chapters—these hats on our heads help set the stage for hilarity and good humor. They remind us to lighten up and enjoy life with our friends, thus following the Red Hat Society's mission of bringing fun-loving women together. Whether we are riding on an amusement park carousel, playing laser tag, or just gathering in the park to blow bubbles, any group of us are guaranteed to spread smiles, and we are certain to be smiling ourselves.

But, if everyone is wearing a hat (and clothing) of the same color, isn't that rather like wearing a uniform? The women of the Red Hat Society are identified with red and purple, but their choices of apparel are anything *but* uniform. You will be amazed and inspired by the creativity and adventurous humor evidenced in these photos and stories about specific Red and Pink Hatters.

Each woman pictured in this book began her "red hat experience" by giving herself permission (and time) to play with her friends. This, in a nutshell, is the premise of the Red Hat Society. Her first red hat was probably fairly subtle, whether she received it as a gift or bought it for herself. But, then...

Like so many Red Hatters do, she decided to take the permission to have fun, granted by membership in the Red Hat Society, seriously—setting herself free to discover all sorts of ways to play. Why not start with the hat itself? What fun to gather ribbons, flowers, rhinestones, glitter, flowers, and tiny strings of blinking lights. And why stop there? Where else can inspiration for embellishment be found? Perhaps in craft stores, magic shops, books, magazines, thrift stores, or shopping malls. Just about anything that can be glued, wired, sewn, or in any way affixed to a hat is a possibility. How might she express her joie de vivre and silly streak right on that hat? She is limited only by her imagination.

Sometimes, over-the-top creations are inspired by truly special occasions, such as a "Reduation," a formal banquet, or a themed hat contest. Red Hatters have risen to all such occasions, demonstrating real resourcefulness and even a touch of

I opted for a conservative queenly topper at the first Red Hat Society convention in Chicago in April 2002.

By August 2002 my hats were making a real statement. They started to get bigger and bolder.

It was another step forward in April 2004, when I wore a red hat bedecked with a beautiful lace veil.

"the crazies." (But, what delicious fun it is to get a little bit crazy now and then!)

Sometimes, a hat is created with a special event in mind. An elegant tea may call for a gorgeous creation of red satin, swathed with yards of tulle and punctuated with silk roses. A chapter outing to the horse races may inspire a bowler with hot-glued plastic toy horses and racing forms on it. Perhaps an Easter bonnet may bear colored eggs and tiny, stuffed chicks—even some bright purple cellophane grass. Our members have been known to create hats such as these—and they're only warming up.

I still smile when I recall the 5-foot-wide red Mexican sombrero, embellished with plastic chili peppers and who knows what else, at a Texas Red Hat Society event, or the Chiquita Banana/ Carmen Miranda concoction seen at our Dallas convention. It really does seem that, once we let our inner little girl come out to play, the sheer joy of unfettered, impulsive creativity takes over. We may often find ourselves smiling, even giggling, as we "work."

An outrageously decorated, colorful hat on our head is where the *real* fun begins. Wearing such a marvelous creation out in public is cause enough, in itself, to set one's playful inner little girl free. And it is impossible to go unnoticed in such an ensemble. You really cannot disappear into the woodwork with a 3-foot-wide picture hat, dripping with sequins, on your head. But, would you want to? There is no doubt that wearing a hat like some of these featured on the following pages helps set the stage for having a wonderful—and *playful*—time.

Won't you please don your own red hat and come out to play?

Sue Ellen Cooper

My hat fashions really picked up with feathers and rhinestones galore in Las Vegas in 2005, where we celebrated the fourth annual Red Hat Society international convention.

By nighttime at the Las Vegas convention I was ready to gamble with my sky's-the-limit red hat.

Now it's "anything goes!" when it comes to my red hat. For an outing at the Boston Tea Party event I chose a sporty red cap.

Table of Contents

> *"When you wear a hat,
> it is like medicine for
> the soul. The hat is the
> expression of who you
> are as a woman in every
> moment! The hat is your
> dreams of who you can
> be. It facilitates the
> different parts of who
> you are: With the wave
> of the hat, voilá! You are
> mysterious... no, you are
> sexy... now proper...
> now playful."* –Anon.

Introduction

It takes chutzpah to wear a hat. It takes nerve, verve, and a bit of devil-may-care attitude to brandish a bowler, flirt in a fedora, or preen in a perfectly primped pillbox.

Oh, heck, that's not true. All it takes is a head and a heart, and perhaps a touch of red for good measure, to get on the hat bandwagon. That's all it's taken for the more than one million members of the Red Hat Society to single-handedly and multi-headedly put head-turning hats back on the runway. And guess what? You are now within the golden circle—you will receive, in chapter after delicious chapter, lots of priceless secrets and tips for making and embellishing truly one-of-a-kind hats. Whether you follow the Hat How-To's or go off on a hatty tangent, you will surely find one or two hats to get your creative juices flowing.

As you work on your enchanting chapeau, keep in mind that you are continuing a centuries-old tradition of hat making. Hats have a fine history, and Red Hatters recognize what ladies took for granted up until a few decades ago—a hat instantly conveys the personality of its wearer to a crowd. It adds style and flair to any outfit. It makes people stand up and take notice. Why, what would the Mad Hatter look like without his zany, outsized top hat?

A Brief History of Hats

There was a time when ladies would not consider stepping foot outside their door without a hat. It was just as necessary as gloves or stockings. Hats conveyed modesty and fashion at the same time. They also conveyed rank; every lady from the queen to the chambermaid wore hats strictly appropriate to her station in life.

Top Hat

In the early days, women generally wore versions of men's hats. Of course, this was well before the time of expert milliners, French ribbons, and glue guns so of course we need to cut these ancestors some slack. It wasn't long—maybe a few hundred years or so—before women started sporting hats of all shapes, sizes, and materials. From then on, a woman's hat was truly a work of art to behold, and she was off! None of this "peacock and peahen" nonsense—women's hats were head and shoulders above men's in their color, variety, and pure aesthetic loveliness, especially when it came to the top hat.

Top Hat

Beribboned Bonnet

By the 1700s, traveling salesmen went all over Europe selling niceties such as straw hat forms, ribbon, and dressmaking notions—they were called Milliners because many of them and their products came from Milan, Italy. The term stuck and became millinery soon thereafter. Milliners turned out handmade hats of both straw and felt, with occasional regal ventures into velvet, silk, furs, and precious metals. Hatmakers made the stiff, conical hat of the English Puritan, the swooping brimmed hats of the swashbuckling pirates, and the sweet, beribboned bonnets of the Empire's elite. They had plenty of business keeping cold heads covered in the days before central heating!

Beribboned Bonnet

Famous Milliners

They are our heroes and heroines, the people who brought hats from the drudgery of pure utility to a wearable art form. We know that someday soon many names of Red Hatters will be added to this venerable list.

• Hattie Carnegie

Carnegie began her career as a trimmer and salesperson in the millinery department of Macy's at the age of 15. Five years later she was a partner in a millinery shop and had changed her name to Carnegie, after tycoon Andrew Carnegie. By 1940 she had expanded into other women's accessories and employed 1,000 people.

• Oleg Cassini

This famous couture designer ventured successfully into millinery. He is especially known as Jacqueline Kennedy's favorite designer, and, indeed, is known along with Halston as the creator of her famous pillbox hats.

• Coco Chanel

Gabrielle was her given name, but Coco Chanel she became—and what a name! She started her career in the 1920s as a Paris milliner before her couture house opened. As her hats were less extravagant than their contemporaries, they caused astonishment due to their stark simplicity, particularly her boaters.

• Lilly Daché

A French-born milliner (1904-1989), Daché apprenticed under Caroline Reboux and Suzanne Talbot before immigrating to the United States to begin a long and luminous career. During her heyday she owned a nine-story building in New York City where her millinery business was housed. It was notable for, among other things, a gold fitting room for brunettes and a silver fitting room for blondes.

Hat with Birds or Feathers

At some point in the late 17th and early 18th century, hats seemed to be for the birds. Or at least, made of birds. Oodles of feathers from exotic species, and sometimes even an entire stuffed bird, would be the ornament of choice on ladies' millinery. Feathers apparently indicated economic prosperity, much like our fancy cars today. The feather fetish got so insane that some birds were becoming extinct and the Audubon Society in the late 19th century stepped in to stop the slaughter. Still, feathers of all sorts continued to embellish ladies' hats until the early 20th century.

Hat with Feathers

Fancy Victorian Hat & Bonnet

By the early Victorian era, France was the place to get the ultimate lady's hat. Milliners on the famed Rue du Faubourg St. Honoré created the finest confections of straw, silk, velvet, and fancy trimmings (which likely included those contraband feathers). As we know from many readings of "Gone with the Wind," even a Southern lady would consider kissing a rake from Charleston if he brought her a hat from that venerable street in Paris.

Bonnets and variations thereof ruled the Victorian age, but by the Edwardian era, hats exploded. Remember the fantastic scene from "My Fair Lady," when Eliza rubs elbows—and enormous hat brims—with the British elite she is trying to emulate? Now those are hats. Even though they were all black and white, these incredible flying saucers literally steal the attention from any other part of the ensemble.

Bonnet

Victorian Hat

Edwardian Hat & Cloche

Yet even as Edwardian ladies paraded in their large hats, a growing number of women were saying, "Forget it—I want to play tennis." An increased penchant for athletics, coupled with World War I, meant that by the 1920s, hats shrank once again. Caroline Reboux, a famous French milliner, is credited with creating the cloche, a low-fitting, narrow-banded hat that looked just right with the bobbed hair and Art Deco craze of the times.

Edwardian Hat

Cloche

Fedora & Turban

Hats remained smaller throughout the 1930s and '40s, but they were still very glamorous. Aided by movie stars like Greta Garbo and Bette Davis, hats were helping to distract people from the Depression and war rations. Beautiful turbans with jeweled brooches, straw pancake hats with silk flower buds, and even felt fedoras to match those tailored suits with enormous padded shoulders kept the mid-century milliners in business.

Fedora

Some economical hatwearer came up with the idea for doll hats, which were essentially miniature hats of a somewhat Victorian style that perched on top of a woman's coiffure.

Turban

• Halston
Halston apprenticed with Lilly Daché in the late 1950s, later designing hats in the famous millinery department at Bergdorf Goodman's in New York. Jacqueline Kennedy's inaugural pillbox is credited to Halston.

• John-Fredrics
This duo, John Piocelle and Frederic Hirst, operated their millinery house from the late 1920s to the late '40s. Their most famous hat was the straw and green velvet bonnet Rhett Butler brings Scarlett O'Hara in "Gone With the Wind" (valued at $20,000 in 1938). They are also credited with popularizing the World War II doll hat.

• Mr. John
After splitting with long-time partner Frederic Hirst in 1948, John P. John, as he had dubbed himself, began a spectacular career making hats for starlets and the fashionable in Hollywood. His hats were very much sought after, and he was also credited with popularizing soft shoulder bags and ballet shoes for streetwear.

• Caroline Reboux

By the mid 1800s, millinery had established itself as being on the same level as haute couture with the first important name in millinery being Caroline Reboux. For more than 50 years, she was one of Paris' leading milliners. Many leading hatmakers of the 20th century trained in her workshops in London and Paris. She is closely associated with the cloche hat of the1920s.

• Elsa Schiaparelli

Elsa Schiaparelli is known for her signature shocking pink hat boxes and cutting-edge designs. Her involvement in the Parisian art world of the 1930s influenced some of her zany hats. She was one of the first milliners to use synthetic fabrics. At one time she employed more than 2,000 people in more than 25 showrooms.

• Sally Victor

Millinery buyer for Macy's in the 1920s before marrying millinery wholesaler Victor Serges. Designed for Serges until starting her own line in the mid-'30s. Her forté was producing quality hats for the masses.

Juliette Cap & Pillbox Hat

Cocktail and church hats from the 1950s also showed beautiful detail and reflected the femininity of the Eisenhower era. Tiny veils and flowers, embroidered juliette caps, and other close-fitting styles had to make way for the enormous beehive hairdos of the 1960s. What to wear on tall hair? Jacqueline Kennedy solved that problem famously with her Oleg Cassini-designed pillbox hats.

Pillbox Hat

Juliette Cap

Lady Diana Hat

Still, style history was emptying the hatbox. By the 1970s, women's hats virtually disappeared. Lady Diana spurred a revival in the 1980s with her captivating personality and matching headwear, but hat wearing has never returned to everyday life. That is until the Red Hat Society burst onto the scene.

Lady Diana Hat

*Red Hat Society—
Anything goes!*

Talking Through Your Hat

To talk through your hat is to talk nonsense, something Red Hatters have turned into a royal art form. Having a happy hattitude is what it's all about. We are always on the lookout for a witty pun and love to play with words. Here is a little history on how hats have made their way into language:

A Feather in Your Cap
A special achievement. In times gone by a feather would be awarded for a special accomplishment and was used to decorate one's hat. A Red Hatter has achieved everything, and may wear as many feathers as she pleases!

At the Drop of a Hat
Fast, immediately. A hat would be dropped to start a race in place of a starting gun. Red Hatters party at the "Drop of a Hat."

Bee in Your Bonnet
Agitation or an idea one cannot let go of. You would have become rather upset if there were a bee buzzing around inside your bonnet! A Red Hatter gets a "Bee in her Bonnet" if anyone tries to make and enforce needless rules.

Eating Your Hat
It means you don't believe something will happen and you are proven wrong. As in if the Exalted Queen Mother ever gets a tattoo, you'll "Eat Your Hat." You better start munching, because she did!

Hat in Hand
To be humble. Probably dates back to when persons of a lower class removed their hats in the presence of a big shot. You won't see Red Hatters "Hat in Hand," for each member is royalty.

Hat Trick
Three consecutive successes. In the past, a cricket bowler who dismissed three batsmen and three balls in a row was awarded a hat. What do you want to guess the hat was named—a bowler?

Trivia with Hattitude

There are so many fascinating facts about hats, we think Trivial Pursuit needs to add a millinery category! We've even put ours in the form of a question, in case a game show ever wants to borrow the detailed facts. To get a leg up, read on.

• What is a hat you'll never find at a dime store?
In the 17th century it was the trend to wear hats embellished with precious gemstones and jewels. Lady Fanshawe, in her "Memoirs," gives a description of the costume of a gentleman at this period (1610), in which a black beaver hat is mentioned, buttoned on the left side with a jewel of 1,200 pounds value.

• What is the Hat Act?
A British law of 1732 restricting manufacture of hats in the colonies to protect and favor the industry in England.

• Who is St. Catherine of Alexandria?
Patron saint of milliners in France, c. 307 A.D., celebrated Nov. 25.

• What is the Royal Ascot?

The world-famous English horse-race meeting at Ascot, dating from the early 18th century, is particularly renowned for Ladies' Day, a unique occasion and setting to flaunt the most spectacular hats.

• Who is St. Clement I?

Third Bishop of Rome, c. 100 A.D. Patron saint of hatters in England, celebrated Nov. 23. By tradition, the discoverer of felt.

• What is a chef's hat?

White, starched bonnet worn by chefs. The tall crown should have 100 pleats.

• What is a wimple?

Head covering worn by nuns, usually of linen or silk, arranged in folds. Formerly worn by other women as well.

Hats Off...

An acknowledgement of success. Somewhere along the line, someone probably suggested something like, "Let's take our hats off to Susan B. Anthony for getting us the right to vote." So the gals all lifted their hats in thanks.

Hold Onto Your Hat

Something big is about to happen! Can't you picture some male driver in a Model T hitting the gas a little too fast and the lady's hat flying off? Thus she learned to "Hold Onto Her Hat!"

Mad as a Hatter

A little silly or nutty. There really was such a thing. Mercury was used in the process of felting hats and the fumes caused hatmakers to exhibit symptoms of being drunk. Fortunately, mercury is no longer used in making hats.

Old Hat

Old, boring, out of fashion. Back when a woman's fashion sense was demonstrated by how up-to-date her hat was, she'd be appalled to be described as "old hat." Red Hatters can be a little sensitive if this term is not used nicely.

Pass the Hat

Literally to pass a hat among a group of people to collect money for charity. Red Hatters have been known to "Pass the Hat" to pay for lunch!

Talking Through Your Hat

To talk nonsense. Red Hatters work hard some days to "talk through their hats."

Throwing a Hat in the Ring

To enter a contest or decide to run for election. It's been surmised that boxers used to "Throw a Hat in the Ring" before a match to signify a challenge. Red Hatters keep their hats on because they are up to the challenge.

Tip Your Hat

The same as "Hats Off," only in this sense of the word you don't have to remove it entirely. A gentle lift of the brim will do.

To Hang Your Hat (or not)

To commit to something or to know for sure. As in you can "Hang Your Hat" on the fact that a Red Hat Society convention is loud and noisy!

Wearing Many Hats

Having many different jobs or duties. Every Red Hatter has worn many hats: friend, daughter, sister, wife, mother, grandmother, volunteer... You get the point!

• What is a "petasi non grata"?

Remember how hoity-toity the familiar Burberry check pattern used to be? It seems that in Great Britain, the Burberry hat has been fervently adopted by the "neds," "yobs," and "20-stone thugs" (translation: non-educated delinquents, young oafs, and really big thugs) and just as fervently became petasi non grata (that's Latin for "an unwelcome hat") among the upper classes.

• What are vanities?

A 15th-century British term for hats.

• What is the difference between man and woman?

Technically a hatmaker makes hats for men while a milliner makes hats for women.

Forming Attachments

For those of you who haven't seen the inside of a crafts store since your last child was in kindergarten, we're here to tell you it's a whole new world out there. With shelves of adhesives, bonding agents, and fusible webbing, a simple matter of sticking one piece of fabric to another can become an exercise in physics and chemistry (something you were also sure you left behind a few years back). Here's a quick primer on what products are best for your hat creation.

Craft Glue

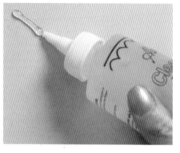

Craft glue is a forgiving, slow-drying tacky adhesive. Typically white or clear in color.

Best used for: A wide variety of applications, from creating your hat accessories to affixing lightweight objects onto the brim or crown.

Notes: Difficult for precision work. Can be a bit messy. Doesn't bond as well as other adhesives on high-pressure points.

Double-Sided Tape

Sold in both dots and strip form, double-sided mounting tape is made with an adhesive that is much stronger than traditional cellophane tape.

Best used for: Used widely in scrapbooking, double-sided tape also works well as a spot adhesive for beads, ribbon, and trim.

Notes: Not intended to withstand heavy wear and tear.

Fusible Webbing

Fusible webbing creates an extremely durable bond with fabric when steam is applied.

Best used for: Bonding two fabric pieces together e.g. hems and appliqués.

Notes: Fusible webbing is available in various strengths, from lightweight to heavy duty. Some are suitable for crafts, others for sewing projects. A steam iron is necessary to create the bond so you need a somewhat flat surface to work on.

Hook-and-Loop Tape

Both hook tape and loop tape have adhesive backing or can be sewn on.

Best used for: Items you want to be detachable or transferable from one hat to another.

Notes: Great adhesion, but bulkier than most other methods. Try hook-and-loop dots for smaller details.

Hot Glue Gun

Glue guns dispense very hot, thin, fast-drying adhesive on fabrics, cardboard, and other materials.

Best used for: Spot adhesion for beads, ribbons, feathers. Good for reinforcing a tight corner or repairing loose items.

Notes: Don't use for entire seams; hot glue doesn't lie flat. Difficult to spread out in a thin layer.

Hot Glue Pellets

Hot glue pellets, beads, or pillows are melted in a skillet or pot, then applied to the surface with a melt-proof scoop or spatula.

Best used for: Applying flowers, beads, and other details to hats.

Notes: You can add color and/or glitter to the glue and stamp it for pretty faux wax seals. Product should not be used around children as pot can easily tip over.

Spray Adhesive

Either temporary or permanent adhesion that is sprayed on a surface. Some sprays have an extended open tack time so that projects can be easily adjusted in place before drying completely. Acid-free formulas are safe for photographs, scrapbook pages, and other memorabilia.

Best used for: Positioning flat, larger objects, such as appliqués, fabric pieces, wide ribbon, etc.

Notes: Not ideal for spot adhesion. Spray on the heavier material and bring the lighter material to its correct position. You can also spray both materials but the bond will be almost instantaneous.

Strong-Hold Adhesive

Better known as "super glue," this instant-drying adhesive creates a very strong bond for paper, fabric, metal, and other materials.

Best used for: Spot adhesion and quick repairs.

Notes: Better be sure you want something in a particular place before applying! These products can be difficult to work with if you're not careful.

Chapter 1

Hoity Toity Crowning Glories

Achieving fame and fortune isn't all that hard. You don't have to join the circus or go on casting calls. You don't even have to get up and do karaoke, the hokey-pokey, or the hoochy-coochy. Nope—that's working way too hard.

Here's what you do: Get up, brush your teeth, get dressed, comb your hair, then put on your darkest faux-designer sunglasses and a drop-dead gorgeous hat. People just assume you're famous when you wear a beautiful hat. And somehow, you start to feel like a celebrity; you become incognito and a standout all at the same time. Everywhere you walk, there is a red carpet. Everywhere you look, people glance at you in admiration. An elegant hat makes a thrift-store dress look like a million bucks. It renders the bad-hair day obsolete. You'll find yourself dressed and out the door incredibly fast because, well, the hat is the outfit.

Those upper-class gals from a century or two ago knew this very well. A young lady could re-do her best bonnet in an afternoon and a gentleman suitor would spend the afternoon wondering how she continued to dazzle him, day after day. So learn from history, and enjoy the fame of an elegant hat. The fortune you'll still have to work on.

"It is the unseen, unforgettable, ultimate accessory of fashion that heralds your arrival and prolongs your departure." —Coco Chanel

Royal Redness Queen Lisa

Lisa Ashby
Strolling Sassy Strumpets
Port Townsend, Washington

As a teenager, Lisa Ashby spent countless hours sewing her latest fashions. She grew up and moved to Alaska, where she designed hats and clothing made with fur.

"I have a creative mind and I get many of my hat inspirations from old books and prints of Victorian fashions," says Royal Redness Queen Lisa. "In one of my past lives, I must have lived during the Victorian era."

Here it is, years later, and Lisa is putting her sewing talents again to good use—as a member of the Red Hat Society. Lisa has made dozens of red hats to fit just about every occasion, often designing some for her Red Hat Society sisters.

Lisa needed a red hat to wear to a regional Red Hat Society convention, and with winter approaching many of the hats she had made in the previous months were too summery. So she got to work by covering a plain red hat inside and out with red velvet. She glued and sewed down all the edges, then cut sections of the netting, which she folded into poufs that were carefully pinned onto the hat in different spots.

Feathers were attached for a fuller effect and then hot glued in place. To finish the hat, Lisa glued another pouf in front and added a sparkly vintage-looking brooch.

"My red hat personality is dynamic and elegant, and still full of mischief. Wearing my red hat draws attention to myself and my Red Hat Society companions, showing how much fun we are having—and that feels great!"
—Lisa Ashby

A Few of My Favorite Things

- Black nylon netting
- Large ostrich feathers
- Rhinestone brooch
- Red velvet

Queen Barbara

Barbara Hoover
Central Valley Red Hat Mamas
Modesto, California

Barbara Hoover always fancied the flair of an ostentatious hat. So when she joined the Red Hat Society she recalled all the things she admired about a hat—a wide brim and classy embellishments—and got to work transforming a straw hat she found at a local nursery.

To create this hat Barbara played around with the positioning of all the materials until the hat expressed her ideas and complemented her face. She pleated a yard of red satin fabric around the base of the crown and secured it with a hot glue gun. Next, she folded ½ yard of black netting until it was doubled, holding the raw edges in one hand and pleating them until the fabric formed the shape of a fan. She glued the netting to the base of the satin fabric band, and then glued red satin roses on top of the netting. Feathers, tucked into the band, were placed on the opposite side of the flowers and netting arrangement. The crowning glory is two rhinestone pins above the satin roses.

- Black feathers
- Rhinestone lapel pins
- Red satin fabric
- Black netting
- Red satin roses

A Few of My Favorite Things

Founding Queenette Ladi Di

Dianne Davis
MZ-TEA-Rious Ladies
Long Beach, California

When Dianne Davis was a girl, she loved to play dress up. Fluffy, colorful dresses, high-heeled shoes, and lots of makeup turned this girl into a sassy young lady. Now that's she's better than 50, Dianne gets to be silly all over—as a member of the Red Hat Society.

Dianne still wears bright colors—red and purple to be specific. She also gets to indulge in period attire.

To transform this basic red straw hat, which she calls her "froufrou hat," Dianne covered the hat with silk fabric then gathered the fabric around the hat, securing it under the brim with hot glue. She then attached tulle to the front, created a pouf at the crown, and attached tulle to the back of the hat. The seam at the back was covered with a tulle bow, its tails running long. Tiny red and purple flowers were glued to the folds of the pouf and to the tail. The finishing touches were all the fun little embellishments, including the bird, beads, feathers, and jewelry.

- Red beads
- Red bird
- Rhinestone pin
- Red tulle
- Ostrich feathers
- Red silk fabric
- Turkey feathers
- Purple and red silk flowers
- Peacock feathers

A Few of My Favorite Things

Queen of the Sierra Sirens

Carlotta Wixon
Sierra Sirens
Grass Valley, California

It usually takes a purple hat to distinguish a Red Hatter in her group. And on this particular day, when she wears her colors in reverse, Queen Carlotta Wixon feels like a regal queen indeed.

"My purple hat sets me apart during my birthday month and says I like wearing feminine things," says Carlotta.

Carlotta took an old straw hat, bought years ago at a discount store, and spray painted it purple. Once the paint dried, she added tulle over the hat, gathering it around the crown and sewing it in place. She then attached it to one side and added grosgrain ribbon around the crown to create a hatband. Next she hot glued and sewed bows, flowers, and feathers in place.

When it's not her birthday, Carlotta loans her purple hat to her friends.

"This hat is also a 'loaner hat' as it has been worn by other members of my chapter during their birthday months," says Carlotta. "I also give each birthday girl a badge with a crown on it to wear that says Queen for the Day."

"Most of us didn't know each other before joining the Red Hat Society, but we are good friends now!"
–Carlotta Wixon

Feathers

Lavender grosgrain ribbon

Lavender tulle

Purple silk roses

Purple spray paint

Sheer purple wire-edge ribbon with gold edge

A Few of My Favorite Things

Founding Queen Mother

Florence Conlon
Classy Red Hatters
Bermuda Dunes, California

Decorating this fanciful red hat became a family affair for Florence Conlon and her daughter, Princess Faith Louise.

One evening, after returning home from a fun dinner gathering with their fellow chapterettes, Florence got inspired to add to her collection of 17 hats. Since she and Faith are both artists, and in business together as doll makers, it wasn't long before their creativity got the best of them.

Florence started with a pair of scissors in one hand and buckram, a stiff moldable cotton fabric, in the other. She started cutting, folding, pinning, and sewing until the hat took shape. Tired but determined, she gathered embellishments she had on hand and, using her glue gun, adhered each item until she achieved a pleasing display.

Diagnosed with a terminal case of pulmonary fibrosis in 2003, Florence has dedicated the rest of her life to having fun with her Red Hat sisters.

"I just wanted something small and casual but classy and elegant at the same time. It sort of just fell together."
—Florence Conlon

Hat How-To

Materials

- Antique belt buckle
- Boning strips
- Buckram
- Chiffon fabric with metallic design: red
- Feathers: red
- Metallic wired ribbon: purple
- Sequin fabric: red
- Silk flowers: purple, red
- Tulle: red
- Wide satin ribbon: red

Instructions

1. To make actual hat base, cut desired size and shape from buckram then cover it with red sequin fabric and bind edges with wide satin ribbon.

2. Bend boning strips in arc shape to hug your head (much like a headband would).

3. Slip boning under ribbon, which is wrapped over to inside, and fasten with hot glue.

4. Once shape takes place, slip one end of red ribbon through large buckle (hat will start to look like a cap shape, so extend and angle sides to hug temples so it just fits over crown of head).

5. Add row of deeply pleated fine red tulle and fasten across back edge so it's standing high.

6. Fold wide strip of red chiffon fabric in half and then glue onto hat to form large double bow; anchor onto center of edge in front of tulle.

7. Fashion two large satin bows and position on each side, with buckle attached so ribbon runs through center of one bow.

8. Pleat tulle and attach to hat; create large triple bow of purple metallic wired ribbon and add to tulle.

9. Glue various sizes and shapes of red and purple flowers so they are cascading down large satin bow on opposite side of buckle; fill in blank areas with red feathers.

Duchess of Betty of Craftsberry

Betty Jean Parker
Spindle City Divas
Cohoes, New York

For some Red Hatters, what comes first—the hat or the hatpin?

With a plain red hat staring her down, Betty Jean Parker knew she could pull off quite a transformation. She stripped the original hat of its tacky decorations and really got to work.

Betty cut three layers of 4"-wide red netting to fit around the crown of the hat three times. She gathered the netting and arranged it on the hat, hot gluing it in place. She tied red satin in place to make the hatband, then layered a row of silk flowers and sequins. Beaded trim was hot glued around the brim and a purple plume was tucked in.

Then Betty was ready for the ultimate challenge—the proper hatpins hand made with a few beads and baubles.

Says Betty Jean, "When I wear my red hat I feel like a 'real lady.'"

"We are a group of 70-plus women with many different personalities who have one thing in common and that is to have the fun we have earned over the years."
–Betty Jean Parker

- Beaded trim
- Purple plume
- Red satin
- Hatpins
- Sequins
- Red netting
- Silk flowers

A Few of My Favorite Things

Divalicious LuLu

LuLu Thomsett
Strolling Sassy Strumpets
Port Townsend, Washington

Every hat that belongs to LuLu Thomsett has a story. And LuLu has a lot of stories.

"Just before packing for a regional Red Hat Society convention, I asked my friend if she had made any purple hats recently in autumn/winter materials," says Lulu. "I had a Mad Hatter motif in mind, and she immediately exclaimed, 'I have the perfect LuLu hat!' "

This particular hat started out as a simple purple affair on the hat-making bench of LuLu's milliner friend, Darlene Startup. Beginning with a large, brimmed straw hat, Darlene cut off the brim, arranged it into a rectangular shape, and then sewed and hot glued it to the crown of the newly shaped hat. The crown was covered with satin, and very fine ostrich feathers were hot glued in place, the ends hand curled with scissors.

LuLu sewed two purple appliqués onto the front of the hat and voilá—a hat fit for a diva was born.

"Darlene said no one else could pull off wearing this hat but me—and I take that as a high compliment," says LuLu.

The LuLu hat, soon dubbed the Queen of Hearts hat, made its way from Washington to the convention in Anaheim, California. It was one of a dozen hats brought down for the festivities.

But don't think LuLu's love affair with hats is fading anytime soon.

"Being a hopeless collector, I realized I had piles of unused fabric, trim, ribbon, flowers, jewelry—you get the idea," says Lulu, who has adorned the majority of her 20-plus red and purple hats. "A rich fantasy life, coupled with lean budgetary restrictions, became a delicious challenge to create the perfect hat from all the little treasures laid before me that over the years of collecting I simply couldn't part with."

"I've enjoyed wearing hats for as long as I can remember. I have always appreciated the artistry of fine millinery as I drooled over fashion magazines, old movies, costume publications, and well-coifed ladies in church."
—LuLu Thomsett

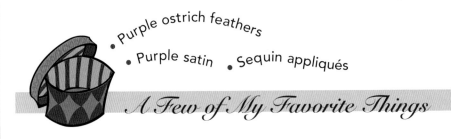

- Purple ostrich feathers
- Purple satin
- Sequin appliqués

A Few of My Favorite Things

Chapter 2

Mad Hatter Tea-Time Toppers

The Red Hatters are a mad bunch. When a Red Hatter attends a tea party, she barely notices the petits fours or the clotted cream. But she will notice every detail on every hat present. In honor of this, we'd like to quote a bit from those crazy characters in *Alice in Wonderland:*

"But I don't want to go among mad people," Alice remarked.

"Oh, you can't help that," said the Cat, "we're all mad here. I'm mad. You're mad."

"How do you know I'm mad?" said Alice.

"You must be," said the Cat, "or you wouldn't have come here."

We know that you wouldn't be reading this chapter if you weren't a bit obsessed with hats. In *Alice*, tea and madness go together in a wonderful, carefree way. That matches our modus operandi to a ... well, to a tea! Tea parties have the undeserved reputation of being staid, fussy affairs where everyone's little pinkie sticks out and no one says anything shocking. Not so in our world—we call it "Red Hatters in Wonderland."

You'll be in fine company with a Tea Party hat that's a little bit (or very, very) silly. Where else in life except among Red Hatters do you get to paste strange objects on your head? This chapter gives you full license to go mad.

"When you wear a hat, it is like medicine for the soul. The hat is the expression of who you are as a woman in every moment." —Anon.

The Diva

Betty DeMars
Red & Pink Hat Mamas
Glendale, Arizona

"My personality is like the red hat I wear on my head—red hot," exclaims Betty DeMars. "My red hat gives me permission and liberty to be me. I can still be a 'child at heart' and my hat allows me to do so."

These days, Betty gets a lot of permission. She decorates all of her hats, usually found on sale at discount stores. Most hats are red but sometimes she'll buy white hats and spray paint them red. Then it's embellishing with whatever strikes her fancy, armed with a hot glue gun.

"I like to be different and unique," says Betty. "I observe other hats but create my own using 'my style.' "

Betty also makes her own purses and clothes to wear to red hat activities. Her chapterettes, all of whom work in the medical field, never know what she'll be wearing.

"The events I attend with my fellow 'sisters' determine what I put on my hats and how I decorate them," says Betty. "These hats allow me to express myself in a creative way."

When it comes to decorating hats, Betty says pile it on. "Gaudy is goofy," she says.

- Children's plastic kitchenware, dishes
- Ribbon
- Sequins
- Silk flowers

A Few of My Favorite Things

Princess Sweet Pea

Patricia Fisher
Crimson Crowns
Anaheim Hills, California

It took her a couple of weeks to find all the pieces, but once she got to work, it wasn't long before Patricia Fisher was hosting a tea party.

A Cheshire cat was invited, as was a little white rabbit. The guests take tea and delight in the decorations atop Patricia's fanciful red hat.

"My hat says I'm creative. It also says I have a silly side and I am secure in who I am."
–Patricia Fisher

A Few of My Favorite Things

- Toy cake
- Plush Cheshire cat
- Glass
- Red silk rose
- Lapel pins
- Toy teacup, saucer, pitcher
- Playing cards
- White rabbit

"We enjoy our '15 Minutes of Fame' during our outings and at traffic stops. Construction workers whistle and people take our pictures. When we play our kazoos in restaurants, other patrons seek requests and managers want to charge an entertainment tax."

—Myrna Johnson

Queen of Mirth

Myrna Johnson
Crimson Belles of Pinellas
St. Petersburg, Florida

"I am the Queen of Mirth, which allows me to become a wild, wacky, wonderful Red Hat Society woman," declares Myrna Johnson, who also enjoys being young at heart.

Myrna found her red hat with a short brim in a costume shop and called on her inner child for inspiration.

The transformation was achieved with a few of Myrna's favorite things and a trusty hot glue gun. She started by gluing Red Hat Society playing cards with teapots around the hat. She then spray painted felt letters and numbers purple, and then attached them to the hat to spell out TEA-4-2. The teacups were hot glued to matching saucers, which were then attached to the brim of the hat. And what's a tea party without cookies? Going one step further with her hat vignette, Myrna hot glued plastic cookies on the brim.

"My hat says that I am special and enjoy being unique," says Myrna. "I may dance to a different drum but I am accepted for being me."

- Purple teacups and saucers
- Felt numbers
- Felt letters
- Plastic cookies
- Purple spray paint
- Playing cards

A Few of My Favorite Things

Lady Lafsalot

Kimberly Rodrigues
Red Hat Ventura Vamps
Ventura, California

Pink Hatter Kimberly Rodrigues purchased this hat several years ago, just waiting for the perfect occasion.

Invited to a Mad Hatter tea party, she remembered that hat and let the theme guide her design.

First she wrapped a pink boa around the hat. She stuffed the plastic teapot, which is incredibly light, with pink tissue paper, then attached ribbon to the spout to mimic steam. The cups and saucers were hot glued to the teapot, which was then embellished with feathers.

Using her computer, she printed Alice in Wonderland characters (cardstock works best), cut them out, and adhered them to pipe cleaners. Curling the ends, she then attached the pipe cleaners to the hat. Curly ribbon tied to the teapot serves as the chin strap to keep the hat in place.

"My hat says I'm wacky, creative, fun-spirited, and willing to pull out all the stops and go over the top," says Kimberly. "I'm just a girl who wants to have fun."

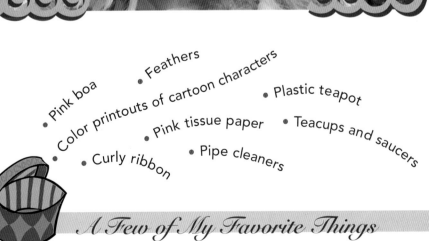

- Pink boa
- Feathers
- Color printouts of cartoon characters
- Plastic teapot
- Pink tissue paper
- Teacups and saucers
- Curly ribbon
- Pipe cleaners

A Few of My Favorite Things

Queen Mariposa

Anna Louise Rodriguez
Imperial Flutterbys
Sacramento, California

"We love to go thrift store shopping but it takes us all day. We start with breakfast about 7 a.m., hit a few stores, lunch, hit more stores, dinner, then a few more stores. Then we're headed home after dessert."
—Anna Louise Rodriguez

Anna Louise Rodriguez started with a plastic tea set from a discount store and ended up with a tea party on her hat.

But that wasn't good enough, so she cut and ruffled a strip of plaid fabric used to cover the brim of the hat, adhering it with hot glue. She cut three lavender lengths of tulle, and two pink lengths, twisted them at the center, and then hot glued them onto the top of the hat to create a hatband.

To attach the tea set, Anna drilled two holes in back of the teapot and cups, and used fishing line to tie everything securely to the hat but the items are still able to wiggle some when she walks. She twirled pipe cleaners and stuck them in the spout, then glued the bunny ears onto each side of the hat. Using a dremel tool to cut a V shape in the bottom of the vase, Anna then attached that to the hat. For fun, she stuck a feather plume in the vase.

"My hat turns my gloomy day into a sassy, fun day," says Anna Louise. "It helps me not give a care what others may think."

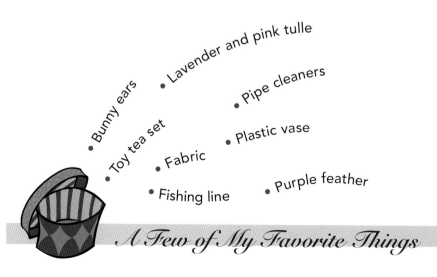

- Bunny ears
- Lavender and pink tulle
- Pipe cleaners
- Toy tea set
- Fabric
- Plastic vase
- Fishing line
- Purple feather

A Few of My Favorite Things

Duchess Flashy

Judy Whitney
Rootin' Tootin' Tooties
Tucson, Arizona

A red hat makes Judy Whitney happy.

Judy and her chapterettes also love a good theme party. So when the idea of a tea party came up she met the challenge with zest—and a hot glue gun.

This very inexpensive hat found at a dime store was covered with satin then embellished with tulle and an assortment of wacky items, including a toy cat, magnifying glass, and a watch.

"I was inspired by my Disneyland adventures as a child," says Judy, "like the Tea Cups ride and Alice in Wonderland tea parties."

Judy has a red hat for every occasion—and in every room in her house.

"I have hats in the attic, on shelves, in the garage, and on dolls—to count them would be a task to say the least," says Judy, who was named Flashy by her chapter soon after she celebrated her 50th birthday and began the hot flashes. "I was in a constant state of flashes, thus the name Flashy."

"We are at our best when we are playing dress up. Give us a theme and we will dress to it. We make everyone we meet laugh or smile."
—Judy Whitney

- Magnifying glass
- Purple tulle
- Red satin
- Purple and red silk flowers
- Tea set
- Purple toy cat
- Watch

A Few of My Favorite Things

Chapter 3

Bra-ha-has & Lampshade Hats

We're just waiting for the day when a certain sexy lingerie company who shall go nameless steals our "wonder-bra" idea. Actually, a nicely made bra (preferably in red) is an excellent base for a shapely hat. Think of it as a red badge of courage.

It takes courage to wear a bra on your head. Secondly, bras are the underclothing of solidarity for most women around the world. Isn't it time we show them off? If beautiful models on TV can flaunt them, why can't we? Third, you can do some amazing millinery feats with a bra.

Then there's the famed lampshade hat—and you don't even need spirits to move you to wear one! From discount stores to lamp stores, Red Hatters are trying these toppers on for size. When they have the perfect fit, it's off to the craft store for feathers and flowers, beads and baubles, and whatever else strikes her fancy. And if the fit is just a little off, you can always hot glue your shade to another red hat and you're off to a good time!

"If a woman rebels against high heeled shoes, she should take care to do it in a very smart hat."—George Bernard Shaw

Vice Queen Gayle

Gayle Christensen
Rascally Reds
Maple Grove, Minnesota

After making two bra purses, Gayle Christensen got to thinking, why not a bra hat to coordinate?

So it was off the chest and onto the head. Gayle grabbed her red 32A and got to work. She started by attaching a flower lapel pin at the front of the bra, and then attached beaded trim around the cups' upper rim. When the hat seemed a bit too big, Gayle attached feathers at the back, making the bra hat fit more securely on her head.

"My hat says I can be as flamboyant as I want and feel so comfortable," says Gayle, who has actually fashioned two bra hats with matching bra purses to date. "I feel I can be me—the one who jumps on a table and dances and feels so alive. My red hat is my real self; it allows me to be me."

Flower lapel pin • Red feathers
• Purple beaded trim
• Red bra

A Few of My Favorite Things

Queen Mary

Mary Kinsey
Rhody Red Hatters
Warwick, Rhode Island

Mary Kinsey is known as the Bra Hat Queen. As long as she can keep everyone laughing, she says they can call her anything they like.

"My bra hat represents fun, happiness, and a sense of humor," says Mary. "I think happy thoughts and I give everyone a laugh and cheer them up when they see my fun hat. I love putting a smile on everyone's face."

To create her bra hat, which is actually two hats in one, Mary hot glued beaded trim and feathers along the bra's support area. She hot glued the bra onto a red hat she had picked up at a discount store, adhered purple satin fabric to the brim, and added a glitter crown at the back of the hat to represent her royal position as Queen. She also added purple roses at the back and purple feather trim along the top of the bra.

"We are a fun-loving chapter full of vim, vigor, and vitality," says Mary. "Our life-size doll, also dressed in a red hat and purple clothes, is named Aunty Dora and we take her to all restaurants and functions. Her hat is a lampshade made into a hat."

Purple feather trim • Red bra • Glitter crown • Purple silk roses • Purple satin fabric • Red beaded trim

A Few of My Favorite Things

Lady Glitz

Carole Steffen
Les Rouge Chapeau
Jackson, Wisconsin
Hat modeled by Polly Laughlin

"Les Rouge Chapeau sisters are known for our hearty laughter, great chocolate appetites, ability to throw a great party together in a few hours, and by our inventive and flamboyant, over-the-top sequined regalia."

–Carole Steffen

She had heard of ladies making bra hats and thought she'd make one of her own. But like all things related to the Red Hat Society, she wanted to take things up a notch.

"For me, the more gaudy, glitzy, and outrageous the better," enthuses Vice Queen Carole, also known as Lady Glitz.

Starting with a red bra purchased at a thrift store, Carole cut off its straps, sewed the back so it would fit her head without falling off, and then cut off the extra band length that had the hook and eye. She added four rows of the boa to fill in the back of the hat, and then sewed a row of sequins under the support area of the bra. Feathers were glued at the top and tassels at each side. The ideal glitzy touch? A rhinestone star pin at the center.

"This hat gives me the right to be out of the wife, mother, grandmother, neighbor mode," says Carole. "I can be silly and come out to play with my friends."

- Red boa
- Red sequins
- Red bra
- Red tassels
- Red feathers
- Rhinestone star lapel pin

A Few of My Favorite Things

"When I put on my red hat, I feel like I belong to a fun-loving group of ladies. I knew those in my chapter but I didn't really get to know them until we became the Bodacious Belles."
—Ruth Lathrop

Queen Ruth

Ruth Lathrop
Bodacious Belles of the Lake
Roach, Missouri

After hearing about the famed bra hats and purses circling Red Hat Society chapters, then seeing one for herself, Ruth Lathrop decided it was her turn to get something off her chest—and onto her head.

So she took a red bra, cut off its straps and removed the underwire, and turned it this way and that way until she got the perfect fit. She then sewed the back closed and hot glued a few red roses to the top.

Says Ruth, "Everyone's always wondering, what will I come up with next!"

- Large red roses
- Red bra
- Red thread

Favorite Things

Crazy Daisies

Joan Taylor
Kay Foster
Margaret Brown
MaryLou Rogers
Carol Ritter
Beaded Babes
Southern California

This group of spirited Red Hatters came up with an ingenious take on the lampshade hat, turning the shade upside down to create a delicious cupcake for a pajama breakfast.

Each gal picked out her own lampshade, spray painted it red, then attached tulle for the chin strip, tied to the wire inside the lampshade. To fashion the purple icing, a 1-yard square of purple lamé was cut and layered with plastic grocery bags. The pouf was closed at the end with a twist tie, then tied to the wire inside the lampshade. A red sequin ornament, attached with a staple gun, makes the cheery cherry on top. Each Red Hatter added her own trim— garland, beads, or lace—under the billowy purple icing.

"The tulle tie makes a great chin lift." –Carol Ritter

- Purple lamé fabric
- Red spray paint
- Red tulle
- Strawberry sequin ornament
- Trim of choice

A Few of My Favorite Things

55

Lady LaDeeDa

Jana Macfadden
Big D Re-Gals
Richardson, Texas

To celebrate their third anniversary, the Big D Re-Gals held a lampshade-decorating contest.

Jana Macfadden took this challenge seriously and sought out a beaded lampshade at a discount store, spray painted it red, and then embellished it with flowers and ribbon secured with a hot glue gun.

Just as fun decorating the hat was looking for the perfect sized lampshade to comfortably fit her head.

"I got the funniest looks when I was shopping for the lampshade with my daughter," says Jana. "I had to try on several lampshades before I found one that would fit my head and stay on. I had to keep asking my daughter how each one looked because there wasn't a mirror around and I could see people giggling and whispering to each other."

She proudly wore the hat to the anniversary party and now it's become, shall we say, old hat?

"I may have a lampshade on my head but I'm wearing it with style and elegance," says Jana, or Lady LaDeeDa in Red Hat Society circles. "My red hat gives me the freedom to be who I truly am inside."

"Every month one of us is Queen for the Day and chooses where we go and what day we meet that month. This makes for a great variety of activities and a few unexpected surprises!"
—Jana Macfadden

- Beaded lampshade
- Red spray paint
- Silk flowers
- Purple wired ribbon

A Few of My Favorite Things

"We wanna bee gaudy
We wanna bee ourselves
We wanna bee disorganized
We wanna bee noticed
We wanna bee friendly
Most of all
We wanna have fun."

—Wanna Bees chapter

- Battery-operated lights
- Plastic scepter
- Silk flowers
- Brooch
- Twirling gig
- Purple and red boas
- Corsage pin

A Few of My Favorite Things

Queen Mudder

Elaine Craig
Wanna Bees
Overton, Texas

When Elaine Craig was invited to a lampshade party, she won a prize for the most unique hat. That's no easy feat, considering there were more than 50 lampshades to choose from.

"The idea for the hat came almost instantly when I saw the twirling light shine the first time," says Elaine.

She found the red lampshade at a discount store and the twirling gig in the children's bike section of another store. She secured boas around both the top and bottom edges of the lampshade with paper clips, hot glued the gig and a scepter to the top, and then added flowers from a corsage her husband had given her one Mother's Day. At the front of the newly fashioned hat she added a bedazzling brooch.

Elaine named the hat "Dis Lil' Light O' Mine" after a Sunday school song she had learned many years ago: "This little light of mine, I'm gonna let it shine. Let it shine. Let it shine."

Queen Pansy

Jeanette Meursing
Primo Purple Pansies
Point Roberts, Washington

"My hat says, in no uncertain terms, that I'm flamboyant to say the least," exclaims Jeanette Meursing.

Leave it up to a Red Hatter to put her thinking (red) cap on to come up with this fun idea. Starting with a colonial-style lampshade picked up at a garage sale, Jeanette spray painted it red, let it dry, and then stuffed the wavy parts of the lampshade with tulle, hot glued in place. To hold the shade on her head, Jeanette hot glued a small hat inside the lampshade, then added tulle ties to each side to secure her newly fandangled red hat under her chin. Finally, Jeanette added a sequin band and assorted embellishments.

"My red hat lets the real me come out and play—and I do play!" says Jeanette.

- Purple butterfly
- Red silk flowers
- Red tulle
- Sequin headband
- Red spray paint
- Purple and red feathers

A Few of My Favorite Things

Chapter 4

Over-the-Top Hats

Once upon a time, there was a little girl (let's just call her Ruby RedHat) who always wanted to be a little bit different from the crowd. She wore bright striped pants with flowered shirts, knee socks with ballet shoes, and huge yarn bows in her hair. One day, her school sponsored a hat contest. Ruby thought and thought—what could she wear? As she watched her mother prepare for dinner, Ruby had a flash of inspiration. The next day, as her friends stared aghast beneath their cowboy hats and baby bonnets, Ruby strutted up the playground in her Chapeau de Cuisine: an upside-down colander loaded with spinach, carrots, and turnips bundled on top. Sure enough, Ruby won first prize for the zaniest hat. Good for you, Ruby!

Not all of us had a nonconformist childhood to be proud of. We might have been wearing the safe cowboy hats and baby bonnets. But Red Hatters stand for nothing if not for the motto, "It's *never* too late to change!"

You can make up for lost time in the prime of your life with the most outlandish hat your imagination can dream up. Studies show that by living out your fantasies and repressed silliness in hat design, you can actually add years to your life! So get going— you have a lot of inner zaniness to express.

"I myself have 12 hats, and each one represents a different personality. Why just be yourself?" — Margaret Atwood

Lady Lawless, Questionable Queen

Lynn Hunter
Corona Cuties
Corona, California

For many years, Lynn Hunter served her community as a police officer.

She's traded in her badge for a red hat and has sworn to uphold the strict guidelines entrusted to her by the Corona Cuties. Those guidelines dictate lots of laughter and minimal seriousness.

Her chapterettes call her Lady Lawless, Questionable Queen and she's out to break the rules when it comes to the ordinary and mundane.

"Being a retired police officer I'm not used to 'blending in' in private life," says Lynn. "My red hat puts me back in the limelight."

When it comes to versatility, her spicy red hat serves many purposes.

Today she's the pillar of Red Hat Society perfection. She's the dancing queen, the Carmen Miranda of the group with her festive turban adorned with a handful of feathers and a queen's crown, all held in place with generous amounts of hot glue.

"I need to cover up my coiffure-challenged hair," says Lynn, "and this hat also makes me look taller."

"If food isn't involved in an activity, nobody goes!" –Lynn Hunter

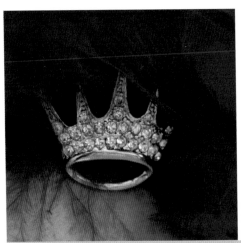

- Crown lapel pin
- Red feathers

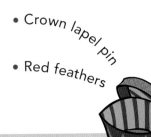

A Few of My Favorite Things

Lady Do-All

Gail Schoenhaar
Scarlett O' Hatters
Garden City, New York

"Wearing my red hat brings out the show-off side of my personality," says Gail Schoenhaar. "There's nothing like getting plenty of attention."

Gail has been affectionately named Lady Do-All since she is always organizing and trying to do everything she can. So when it came time to dress for a Mad Hatter tea, she lived up to her nickname.

To create her show-stopper, Gail glued a boa around the outside of her red straw hat, purchased at a local fabric store, then glued Queen and King of Hearts playing cards onto the crown. She painted wooden hearts and added those too, then attached metal jacks all around the hat and onto the wooden hearts. A couple of gift boxes and a few bows on top and Gail was just about done. For fun, she added the pompom trim around the edge of the brim as the perfect finishing touch.

"The funniest comment I've received when wearing this hat was at the Belmont Racetrack," says Gail. "A gentleman there said he'd rather watch me prance around than the horses."

- Bows
- Metal jacks
- Purple metallic bows
- Purple pompom fringe
- Playing cards
- Red boa
- Small gift boxes
- Purple and red wooden hearts

A Few of My Favorite Things

Her Royal Hiney Queen Linda

Linda Neas
Fabulous Fruitcakes
Portsmouth, Virginia

"The idea for my hat came from my desire to make a hat that would represent the silliness of my Red Hat Society chapter, the Fabulous Fruitcakes," says Queen Mother Linda Neas. "What better symbol that a Red Hatter in full regalia having fun by popping out of a fruitcake?"

Linda was not short of humor when she designed this red hat.

"My red hat says I am totally alive and 'kicking,' " says Linda. "I am not afraid to explore all the fabulous fun and adventure that life has to offer. I'm going for the gusto, and I'm taking my Red Hat Society sisters along for the ride."

"Our chapter tries to do things that are different. We have gone on a hayride to a pumpkin patch, a trip to the zoo, a boat ride at the Botanical Gardens, a Red Hat Society pottery-painting party, and a picnic with games like pantyhose golf. We celebrate silliness at every turn." –Linda Neas

Hat How-To

Materials

- Acrylic paint: black, flesh color
- Cording
- Craft glue
- Decorative trim
- Doll wig
- Glitter: red
- Heavy-duty tape
- Hot glue gun
- Marabou trim
- Muslin doll
- Paintbrushes
- Plastic fruit
- Poster board
- Red hat
- Satin fabric: purple, red, white
- Wire

Instructions

1. To create cylindrical cake form, cut rectangular piece of poster board and shape into column for cake's sides, making sure "cake" is sized to sit on red hat.

2. Cut round piece of poster board for top.

3. Using heavy-duty tape and wire reinforce inside bottom, sides, and top of cake form.

4. Cut white satin fabric to cover sides of cake; hot glue in place.

5. Cut hole in cake top; insert doll so it appears to be popping out of cake to check for placement.

6. Paint muslin doll body with flesh-color acrylic paint; with thin brush and black acrylic paint, draw facial features.

7. To dress doll, wrap purple fabric and ribbon around doll's body and secure with hot glue. Gather top of dress fabric into rosette and hold in place with rubber band.

8. Hot glue doll wig, fabric shoe, and leg in place.

9. Working on top of cake, cut scallops of red satin fabric to resemble frosting and hot glue in place; apply decorative trim to cover edges of cake.

10. Cut circle of red satin and turn edges under at top of cake. Cut hole in center of satin top for the doll; place doll on top of cake with free leg pulled into cake form for stability.

11. Hot glue doll in place, and then fit red satin cake top to cover all edges.

12. Add decorative fruit, then write birthday message with craft glue and glitter on separate banner of silk and glue to cake.

13. Add marabou boa; secure to hat form with hot glue.

Lady Flutterby

Sandra Ingraham
The El Monte Yacht Club
El Monte, California

Sandra Ingraham is a self-proclaimed hat fanatic. Every time she opens a magazine or catalog she's always looking for the next best idea to dress up her hats.

To date she has more than 30 hats and just as many hatboxes.

"I love wearing hats and always to church," says Sandra. "I am usually the only one with a hat on nowadays."

Sandra's red hat came in first when her chapter held a contest to decorate a net hat.

"I made it from scratch!" she says.

To begin, Sandra shaped her netting to fit her head and sewed it in place. She then put butterfly clips all around the hat then added large feathers and a couple of silk roses. Two strings of plastic beads were added, one on each side.

"I love this hat and I love making my hats different each time," says Sandra.

- Beaded garland
- Butterfly clips
- Red netting
- Feathers
- Silk roses

A Few of My Favorite Things

Diva of Distractive Design

Patti Pierce
Rosy Riveters
Montebello, California

When Patti Pierce wears her red hat, she's honoring the millions of Rosey the Riveters who took over the jobs men left behind when they headed off to World War II.

"The women actually started a female revolution that led to many major changes," says Patti. "Three we acknowledge are the beginning of the day care system, the 24/7 grocery store, and the wearing of pants as a fashion statement."

To symbolize the women's dedicated efforts, Patti picked up a hard hat at a local home improvement store.

"Originally white, I sprayed the hard hat with plastic primer then added several layers of red spray paint," says Patti. "I then brushed the hat with glitter glue and added many layers of spray gloss sealer."

The artist's palette was cut out of a thin piece of oak. Each glitter color was added with glue then allowed to dry. The brush tips were dipped in glue then in red glitter, and adhered with industrial-strength craft glue. The model plane, a metal P-38 Lightning World War II bomber, was painted white, brushed with craft glue, and sprinkled with glitter.

"The real WWII bomber was designed in 1939 and put in production in 1941," says Patti. "It was famous for its unique design, speed, and ability to achieve altitude during the war. There were probably many 'Roseys' who worked on the plane."

- Art brushes
- Model airplane
- Artist's palette
- Red glitter glue
- Red spray paint
- Assorted colors of glitter
- Spray gloss sealer

A Few of My Favorite Things

"Our members started as strangers and have since developed a loving, warm camaraderie. We have fun being innovative, creative, and resourceful. We are using our talents and histories to the fullest."
—Patti Pierce

Queen Sherry

Sherry Swan
Westminster Royal Belles
Westminster, California

When Sherry Swan decided she would attend the International Red Hat Society convention in Las Vegas, she just had to have the perfect hat.

Not just any hat, mind you, but a hat with all the glitz of Sin City.

"So I commissioned my girlfriend's stepdaughter to make me a hat with a Las Vegas theme," says Sherry. "Danyel is an extremely talented artist and up until this time she had designed only paper party cone hats."

What they came up with for the basic red hat were Queen playing cards in four suits, large jewels befitting her majesty, ribbon with a card theme, feathers, and netting. But the crowing touch, says Sherry, is the lighted Las Vegas sign.

"My hat says that I am outgoing, bold, colorful, and over the top," says Sherry. "I am willing to gamble and venture 'outside the hatbox.'"

"A red hat is magical and makes me know that I can be and do anything. It is an expression of who I am." –Sherry Swan

- Las Vegas sign
- Queen playing cards
- Black, purple, and red feathers
- Red netting
- Gold and red glitter
- Red sequins
- Gold filigree
- Ribbon with card theme
- Good Luck sign
- Small club, diamond, heart, and spade ornaments
- Large amethyst, diamond, and ruby faux jewels

A Few of My Favorite Things

Madame Le Bon Temps Roulet

Margaret Brown
Beaded Babes
Buena Park, California

If Margaret Brown knows anything, she knows how to dance. She also knows how to kick up her heels and onto her hat.

Dancing since was 3 years old, Margaret still competes and performs. Her hobby inspired this fun 4-pound hat.

"The idea for my 'Legs Art' was inspired by my love of dance and having a good time at loving what I do," says Margaret, whose regal name is Madame Le Bon Temps Roulet (French for Let the Good Times Roll). "My name says it all."

Hat How-To

Materials

- Bias tape: red
- Cyclist helmet: foam
- Fish line: 20 lb.
- Fishnet stockings: black
- Lace seam tape: black
- Lamé fabric: red
- Leather granny boots: red
- Mannequin legs
- Netting: black, red
- Ribbon laces: red
- Straw hat: red

Instructions

1. Place helmet on head; position legs in a kicking position toward front of helmet to balance them to figure out placement. With sharp knife, burrow out enough room to nestle in knees of mannequin legs; set aside legs to attach later.

2. Fit helmet on straw hat to size; cut brim off straw hat and adhere to bottom edge of helmet with hot glue.

3. Hot glue red lamé to cover helmet; cut out two holes for legs to fit through.

4. Cut two to three 5″ x 72″ strips of red netting; sew edge with red double-folded bias tape. Run gathering stitch through center of red netting strip to create double ruffle for girl's skirt; hot glue along gathering stitch and adhere to brim of straw hat.

5. Cut 3″ x 36″ strip of black netting; sew with black lace seam tape and fish line so ruffles will stand. Run gathering stitch through center of black netting strip to create double ruffle for girl's underskirt; hot glue to top of helmet.

6. Slip stockings over mannequin legs; hot glue at tops of legs to keep in place. Hot glue tops of legs, turn over, and adhere to top of helmet. Slip boots on feet and tie laces with red ribbons.

7. Cut 1½ yards x 3″-wide piece of red lamé fabric. Finish edges with rolled hem, run gathering stitch down middle of fabric, and gather (forming double ruffles). Hot glue, along gathering stitches, to top of helmet to fill in space around legs.

La Reine Mere De Domsront

Sue Denny
Red Hat Society of Normandy
Domfront, Normandy, France

In France, where Sue Denny lives, the Red Hat Society helps her meet other English ladies living in her area. She figures, what better way to shout to the world, "I'm here!" than with a red hat?

Sue had this hat for many years before she joined the Red Hat Society. To craft this creation, she cut a hatband out of felt, attached it to the hat, and then added the netting and feathers. To show her patriotic spirit, she embellished the hat with a few images of her native country, in addition to photos and postcards of France, all secured to the hat with lapel pins.

"The hat represents my two countries—England, with images of Big Ben, a post box, and a London bus—and Paris—with pictures of the Eiffel Tower on Millennium night and the beautiful Sacre Coeur," says Sue. "The netting and feathers represent the Moulin Rouge."

"Our first chapter meeting was to be a garden party at my home. After a long trip, I returned home to find the garden under weeds 4½ feet high. Change of plans. The day was so hot that we retreated indoors for lunch with the shutters closed and our purple dresses clinging to our perspiring bodies!" –Sue Denny

- Lapel pins
- Red felt
- Red netting
- Photographs
- Photographs
- Postcards
- Red feathers

A Few of My Favorite Things

2.M. Judimouse

Judi Winderweedle
Disney Darlings
Carlsbad, California

"My hat says I love to have fun and I love to laugh," exclaims Judi Winderweedle, whose affection for red hats is contagious.

"I love to take women who say they look awful in a hat on hat-buying trips," she says. "I tell them, 'You need to wear the hat, not the hat wear you.' A tilt of the hat or a little bend of the brim can make all the difference in how a hat looks on. There is a hat for everyone out there somewhere. You just need to take the time to find it."

Judi found her hat at a costume store after joining the Red Hat Society some years ago. Feathers were arranged on the side of the hat then secured with hot glue. A large glittered rose that had decorated the birthday cake of her friend's mother was strategically placed in the center, completely transforming this plain hat. The beauty is now well suited for an elegant garden party.

• Purple and red feathers

• Silk rose

A Few of My Favorite Things

Princess of Too Much Fun

Darlene Durbin
Last of the Red Hat Mamas
Lake Havasu City, Arizona

Nursery rhymes and fairy tales can spur the imagination in children and Red Hatters alike.

When it came time to get ready for a Red Hat Society gathering at Disneyland in Anaheim, California, Darlene Durbin looked to Alice in Wonderland to create a unique red hat for the Mad Hatter Tea Party.

"I am the Princess of Too Much Fun," says Darlene, "and this hat reflects that. It makes me happier than my usual happy."

To create the hatband, Darlene covered a headband with craft glue and added felt cut into ears, a tail, and a Cheshire cat smile. She then tucked a few feathers into the hat, which was given to her by a dear friend who has a very old collection of hats.

"She gave me the hat because she knew I was a Red Hatter and I would do something fun with it," says Darlene.

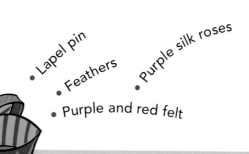

- Lapel pin
- Feathers
- Purple silk roses
- Purple and red felt

A Few of My Favorite Things

Chapter 5

Little Critters Chapeaux

Don't worry—these are not *real* critters! We're strange but not that strange. We just love how insects, birds, and cute little animals look perched on top of our heads.

Picture it: a bevy of butterflies fluttering around your hat will make you the Most Popular Red Hot Mama of all times. Do you raise golden retrievers? Are horses your passion? Batty for bats? Think of your head as an empty parade float. Then, imagine a menagerie taking shape. We have fond memories of a head-top rendition of "The Goose Who Laid the Golden Egg." (Just remember to stay away from duck hunting areas.)

One lady with a fabulous collection of jeweled frog brooches grieved because they just sat in a dark drawer. Once she came out of the "hat closet," she joyously adorned each and every hat with a flashy frog. She even created lily pads out of green velvet. See how easy it is?

Using images of animals on clothing has a long history, portraying woman's instinctive response to the natural world surrounding her. It's also a great way to meet people. Wear a hat peppered with penguins to your next social gathering and you can be sure all eyes will be on you. Someone might even be brave enough to strike up a conversation.

"Leave everyone wondering which is the more interesting piece of work … you or your hat." —Anon.

Queenmummy

Carol Ritter
Beaded Babes
Fullerton, California

Carol Ritter has an infinite number of hats, thanks to her ingenious interchangeable design.

The secret to her expandable wardrobe is a straw hat fitted with two pieces of fabric sewn with elastic, one cut to fit the brim and the other cut to slip over the crown. Embellishments are added with corsage pins and thus a garden hat is born—or a bunny hat or a Victorian-inspired hat.

"I have attended all the Red Hat Society conventions so far, and I only have to travel with one hat and one box of embellishments. I've even made a purple brim and crown cover to use during my birthday month."
–Carol Ritter

Hat How-To

Materials

- Boa
- Butterflies
- Craft bird
- Elastic: ¼″ wide
- Feathers: purple, red
- Hatpins
- Jewelry
- Lace
- Ostrich feathers
- Ribbon
- Satin: red
- Silk flowers

Instructions

Brim Cover

1. Measure outer edge of hat brim and add 4″; cut fabric to length.

2. Measure from where crown and brim meet on top to underneath where brim and crown meet; add 2″ and cut fabric to this width.

3. Put right sides together and sew seam connecting two ends, making circle of material.

4. On each edge, turn under and sew ½″ channel, leaving slight opening to insert ¼″-wide elastic.

5. Insert 48″ long piece of elastic.

6. Fit brim cover over hat brim, adjusting elastic to make cover gather and fit snuggly at bottom of crown.

Crown Cover

1. Cut 25″ circle; sew leaving 2″ opening to turn fabric inside out. Turn right sides out and press.

2. Stitch line completely around piece 2″ from outside edge of circle.

3. Stitch second line 1½″ from outside edge, leaving slight opening to match outer opening where you turned circle; insert 24″ piece of ¼″-wide elastic.

Hat Band

1. Sew your choice of material into circle. Slide hatband into place where brim and crown meet.

2. Attach embellishments with corsage pins, hatpins, or small stapler.

Lady Emerald

Carolyn Storms
Sweet and Sassy Gals
Sun City West, Arizona

She doesn't know the measurements for the fabric, correct millinery terms, or the amount of hot glue it takes. Carolyn Storms just knows how to embellish hats.

Carolyn, whose hobby is floral designing, purchased a dragonfly with the idea of using the ornament outside near her window boxes. It never made it outside, but it eventually found its way onto her first red hat.

Fifty hats later, Carolyn considers this the hat that started it all.

"Wearing this hat," says Carolyn, "I feel like royalty."

To transform this inexpensive ready-made hat, Carolyn covered the top with purple satin and hot glued it in place. With a long length of pre-cut gathered lace, she covered the brim and then added purple flowers.

At the back of the hat, two long pieces of red lace were hot glued in place to create streamers, their edges accented with gold and red fringe. Carolyn took about two yards of netting in her hands, formed it into a billowy shape, tacked it with red thread, and then pinned it to the hat.

Says Carolyn, "I never sew or hot glue anything in place until I pin it first to check the position. I keep glue to a minimum as it adds weight to the hat; sew whenever possible."

- Fabric dragonfly
- Gold and red fringe
- Red lace
- Purple satin
- Red netting
- Purple silk flowers

A Few of My Favorite Things

Vice Queen

Anita Medford
L.O.V.E. Red Hats
Middleburg, Florida

"I love to see the smiles on people when our group walks into a room," says Anita Medford. "I can always count on laughter when I see a red hat."

She may be thinking it's her chapter that is causing the giggles, but chances are it's her hat. Peeking out of her red hat, which she wrapped with leaves, netting, feathers, and flowers, is a smiling yellow cat.

"I'm a cat lover and an avid cat collector; my grandchildren were excited to see the stuffed cat they had given me perched on my head," says Anita. "I love all things with cats and own several Red Hat cat T-shirts, and I needed a hat to match."

- Faux jewels
- Purple and red silk flowers
- Large purple feathers
- Light purple netting
- Silk leaves
- Stuffed cat

A Few of My Favorite Things

Lady Lifesaver

Connie Buzbee
Bling Bats in Red Hats
Sacramento, California

When it comes to sparkles, Connie Buzbee says her chapter has the rest beat.

"We are the blingiest bunch of ladies in the area," says Connie, who puts a shimmer in everything she wears.

While this hat was not designed around the rhinestone spider, "he just jumped on board for the ride," says Connie.

This store-bought purple hat got its transformation with 4″ fringe around the top and lots and lots of feathers hot glued around the hat.

- Fringe
- Purple and red feathers
- Rhinestone spider pin

 Favorite Things

Queen Mother

Nan Ide
Rockin' Rubies
Zillah, Washington

Having a good time is something to chirp about. Just ask Nan Ide, who puts a little fun into everything she does.

"When I wear this hat I feel beautiful and also slightly silly," she says, a bird chirping atop her head.

For fun one afternoon Nan attended a hat-making workshop. It inspired her to attempt her own creation and after a month of due diligence, she was ready to don her new red hat.

She started with an inexpensive floppy hat form. Hers is paper, though she says straw would work well too. With a needle and thread she sewed lace around the brim and padded the crown with bubble packing material covered with red satin. She layered the satin with lace, hiding the seams with silk flowers and tulle.

Since the hat seemed a bit too floppy for her taste, Nan added a plastic holiday wreath form underneath the brim and disguised it with more tulle. She then added jewels, flowers, bows, feathers, hatpins, and a cardinal that chirps.

Says Nan, "Sometimes a little too much is just enough."

"The Rockin' Rubies are dedicated to Country Western line dancing and we offer lessons, demonstrations, and fun. We have chapter members in Washington state, Nevada, Michigan, and Texas, and we're recruiting more joyful dancers wherever we go."
—Nan Ide

- Artificial chirping bird
- Feathers
- Red lace
- Bubble packing material
- Red satin
- Hatpins
- Red silk flowers
- Faux jewels
- Plastic wreath form
- Red tulle

A Few of My Favorite Things

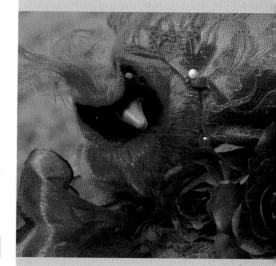

"We're called 'Joyful Noise' because that's what we make when we're together!" –Annie Humke

- Feather hat band
- Large butterfly

Le Baroness de Bling

Annie Humke
Joyful Noise
Tustin, California

Annie Humke was celebrating her 25th wedding anniversary on a road trip north of San Francisco when she spotted something so unique, so unusual…and so big. It was a gigantic red fabric butterfly and she just couldn't resist.

An admirer of these fluttering beauties, Annie didn't know what she would do with it but she knew she just had to have it. She plunked down a few bucks on the counter as her husband patiently waited nearby.

When she returned home she remembered she had an inexpensive red hat she'd picked up a year before at a local swap meet. She decided the two should meet, introduced a feather hatband, and voilá—a dynamic red hat was born.

"I had seen a big butterfly on another Red Hatter some time ago and I thought it was fabulous," says Annie, Le Baroness de Bling. "This hat gives me wings to fly. Why hang around hooked to terra firma, you know?"

Madame Butterfly

Chris Kentera
Chapeaux Rouge
Salt Lake City, Utah

Chris Kentera was deemed the Queen of Halloween when she showed up at a Witches Tea wearing this frightful yet delightful red hat.

"On Halloween my hattitude is particularly devilish because my birthday is Oct. 31," reveals Chris. She nicknamed this her "phobic hat" as she dislikes spiders immensely.

"Maybe that's why I chose to 'play' with them," she says.

Chris purchased this straw sombrero at a party store and spray painted it red. She wrapped the hat with tulle and covered the crown with plastic spiders, and then suspended one of the spiders from plastic fishing line to give the illusion of a spider on a web. The large wire spider in the center of the hat was a special gift from a friend.

Says Madam Butterfly, "Lots of spiders with plenty of red and purple thrown in makes the hat pretty in spite of the creepy, crawly critters."

- Large wire spider
- Plastic fishing line
- Plastic spiders
- Red spray paint
- Purple tulle

A Few of My Favorite Things

Queen Know it All

Cathy Kiley
007 Red Hats
Folsom, California

If there's anything that can make a Red Hatter laugh, it's a silly red hat.

And for some, a silly outfit to match.

"This hat makes me feel special; it lifts my spirits and encourages me to have fun and joke around," says Cathy Kiley, wearing a Minnie Mouse-style dress.

Cathy sent away for this Mickey Mouse Club hat when she was a young girl. As she grew older she tucked it away, and it survived several moves over the years. Wearing her thinking (red) cap, she decided it was time to bring it out again.

To make over her hat, Cathy simply removed the club seal from the front of the hat, spray painted it red, and sprinkled on spoonfuls of glitter. She then replaced the seal with a little craft glue.

- Red glitter
- Red spray paint

Favorite Things

Kween Karen

Karen VanHook-Gross
Lively Ladies of the Lake
Allyn, Washington

Karen VanHook-Gross wanted something big and showy to wear for the Red Hat Society International Convention in Las Vegas.

Karen was traveling by plane to the convention so she needed a hat that could travel with her. When designing her hat, she tucked the 12 tall ostrich feathers into a stretchy hatband, which was made removable by using hook-and-loop tape.

To make the base of the hat, Karen attached batting to the crown with craft glue, enough to make it puffy. She formed the fabric over the crown and brim and glued and stitched it in place. Next she draped the beaded garland over and around the hat, tacking it in place with fabric glue. Final embellishments included artificial roses and a clip-on butterfly.

"My red hat says I am outgoing, creative, silly, and somewhat flamboyant, willing to be noticed," says Karen. "I like to meet new friends and I like to play hard."

- Artificial roses
- Fabric
- Sequin stretch band
- Batting
- Ostrich feathers
- Clip-on butterfly
- Red beaded garland

A Few of My Favorite Things

Queen Mother Shirley

Shirley Blair
Hippie Hatters
Noblesville, Indiana

> "We just love spending time together and having fun. We are a true sisterhood— 'all for one and one for all.' We lift one another up."
>
> –Shirley Blair

Shirley Blair wanted a red witch hat for Halloween. She found this hat online and when it arrived, she knew it just wouldn't do.

So she got to work adding a string of feathers around her regal hat. And that just got her creative juices flowing. Shirley went on a hunt for elements befitting her Queen Mother status, including a purple spider to celebrate the holiday. The spider was hung from the crook of the hat with floss, which was sewn onto the top. Two sequins were glued onto the floss to hide the sewing knot. On one side Shirley pinned a flashing cat pin, a hatpin, and a red fluffy puff pin. On the other side she added a red plume held in place by a "bling" pin. A small crown pin was added to the front, and a marabou fluff under the headband finishes off the hat.

"My chapterettes love to see how my 'next hat' will be embellished," says Shirley. "My hat says, 'She must be a lot of fun—look at that hat!' "

Crown, flashing cat, fluffy puff, and rhinestone lapel pins

- Embroidery floss
- Red plume
- Hatpin
- Marabou
- Purple feathers
- Red sequins
- Purple pompom spider

A Few of My Favorite Things

Duchesse of Crimson

Ann Nickerson
Serendipity Sisters
Snohomish, Washington

Red hat shopping is not just for Red Hatters; some of their family is getting in on the fun too.

Ann Nickerson's husband and daughter often return home with a hat or two in hand, including this peacock hat found at a thrift store. To date, she has decorated more than 70 hats.

"Any color, any shape—they continue to track down hats that need my help," Ann laughs, cheerfully taking on such challenges so that she may have a red hat on hand for anyone who needs one. "Each hat seems to dictate how best to enhance its potential beauty."

To bring out the beauty of this hat, Ann spray painted it red and let it dry in the sun. She glued red boa feathers around the hat, and added a peacock feather found among Christmas decorations. Ann then dressed up the bird's tail with beads and more feathers.

"I wore this peacock hat to a Red Hat Society convention," says Ann, the Duchesse of Crimson. "On banquet night, I stood by the elevator feeling gorgeous. I was asked by another Red Hatter, who was also waiting, if she could take my picture. I was thrilled and said yes, of course. Then she asked me to bend down. She only wanted a picture of my beautiful red hat!"

"My hats tell others that I have a sense of style, a dash of daring, and a pinch of eccentricity. They also make me feel recognized as part of a very special group of women."
—Ann Nickerson

- Beads
- Feathers
- Purple and red ribbon
- Red boa
- Peacock feather
- Red spray paint

A Few of My Favorite Things

Chapter 6

Blooming Brims

Next time you're out strolling in your garden, remember the tender words of Tennyson as he urged his sweet Maude, "Queen rose of the rosebud garden of girls, Come hither, the dances are done…"

Now for all you bards of the hat persuasion, it's time to practice poetry on your head, letting Nature be your muse. Real flowers or silk, a single three-leaf clover or an entire flowerpot, you will be communing big time with Mother Nature in your one-of-a-kind garden hat. Whether they're sweet daisies, bodacious roses, or ripened fruit, gifts from the garden make stunning embellishments to hats large and small.

For those of you who get a kick out of still-life paintings, here's a news flash: Fruits and vegetables make excellent hat décor as well. After all, that's how Carmen Miranda became a household name. We don't know what the language of fruits and vegetables is, but we do know it's best to go faux—you don't want fruit flies ruining your grand entrance.

"When you wear a hat, it is like medicine for the soul.

The hat is the expression of who you are as a woman in every moment!

The hat is your dreams of who you can be." —Anon.

Royal Needleworker to Queen Linda

Molly Sigal
Rowdy Red Hat Mamas
Eagan, Minnesota
Hat modeled by Kay Foster

> *"The most fun part of our group is playing dress-up with Queen Linda Glenn. Her Secret Treasury allows even very limited income sisters to participate in whatever she thinks up next—a parade, a garage sale, community shelter event, a theater outing, and of course, tea."*
> —Molly Sigal

When Molly Sigal thought about designing her own hat, she recalled the graciousness of Audry Hepburn and the elegant costumes of "My Fair Lady."

With a very old photograph of her friend's grandmother wearing a wide-brimmed hat in hand, Molly set out gathering pretty things for her birthday chapeau. She unearthed a favorite purple hat with a sturdy brim from her closet and grabbed her hot glue gun. To begin, she attached a block of floral foam to the hat, folding up the brim to cover it. She added small flowers to the front and clouds of red and purple ribbons "puddled" strategically and "pouffed" as needed. Light and dark variations of the garland were intertwined with large silk flowers, which were then hot glued to the hat.

"Three pheasant feathers," says Molly, aka Lady Marylynn, "feed my asymmetrical soul."

- Beaded garland
- Floral foam
- Pheasant feathers
- Purple and red vintage ribbons
- Large and small silk flowers

A Few of My Favorite Things

Queen of Confusion

Pamela Dove Hasson
MZ-TEA-Rious Ladies
Anaheim, California

Pamela Dove Hasson feels a bit out of place in the 21st century.

"I should have been born during the mid to late 1800s," reveals Pamela, who, for the past two decades, has made costumes styled from this period. She and her husband are characters at Calico Ghost Town in Barstow, California. "Because of the hats I make to match my costumes it was an easy transition to make a red hat."

Starting with a basic red hat, Pamela covered the form with chiffon and satin fabric, using a gathering stitch to secure the fabric that covers the brim around the crown. The fabric is wrapped under the brim and attached inside the brim with a few stitches. Accessories were both sewn onto the hat and attached with a hot glue gun. Once the base of the hat was decorated, Pamela added ribbons and flowers, then attached smaller elements like jewelry, birds, doilies, horsehair, and fruit.

"A little or a lot—depends on how over-the-top you want to flaunt," says Pamela.

"I love planning events. We've had a Nevada Stateline bus trip with lots of prizes and food and Red Hat scarves for everyone; a dinner theatre outing; and a Stepford Wives Brunch where we lunched and munched, hit a few stores, then watched 'Stepford Wives' at a local movie theater."
—Pamela Dove Hasson

- Craft birds
- Red chiffon fabric
- Lavender and purple horsehair
- Velvet roses
- Red satin fabric
- Vintage doilies
- Vintage jewelry
- Plastic berries and grapes
- Various colors ribbon

A Few of My Favorite Things

Red Goddess

Deborah Ford
Santa Teresa Red Hots
San Jose, California

For years, Deborah Ford watched the fancy hats and the fun hats. She bought herself a red hat and continued her studies of what made a pretty garden hat.

She picked up some feathers here and some fabric roses there, without a real plan in mind.

"I'm creative," says Deborah. "I like feathers and big hats and standing out in a crowd."

To fashion this beauty, Deborah rolled a piece of velvet into a hatband then hot glued it in place. She inserted the feather before the glue set and added the purple fringe. Another feather was wound around the hat and fastened with a lapel pin. Velvet roses were attached to the band, which was embellished with a few more feathers.

When she's wearing her hat, Deborah says, "I feel like I'm saying, 'Hey, everybody! I'm over 50 and still full of life and fun!' "

"We have the best Queen. She has a crown, scepter, and cape. She's beautiful."
—Deborah Ford

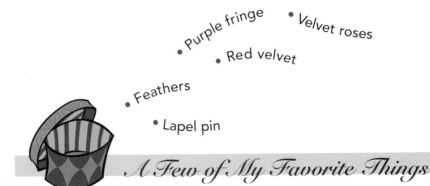

Purple fringe • Velvet roses
• Red velvet
• Feathers
• Lapel pin

A Few of My Favorite Things

Judy of England, Queen of Norbys

Judy Huitt
Norbys Red Rowdies
Anaheim, California

It takes a thoughtful Red Hatter to meet the needs of her chapterettes.

"My ideas for this hat came from listening to fellow members who said a big hat was great for teas, but too hot when going to concerts in the park," says Judy Huitt, who was born and raised in England and thus named Judy of England, Queen of Norbys. "They did not want something that was plain or ordinary."

But rowdy, that she could do.

"My chapter was going to a comedy club and I wanted a red hat that wouldn't be in anyone's way," says Judy. She also wanted something classy yet casual.

So she bedecked an everyday headband in red refinery and then set about creating another 27 for each member in her group.

"What's great about this hat is that it's not hot on the head and it doesn't easily blow off," she says.

Judy started with a red headband, which she covered with a boa. She hot glued red and purple feathers around a big red rose at the front of the hat, then finished it off with a few rhinestones added to the feathers and rose petals.

Says Judy, "When we are in public wearing our colors we always bring out the best in others."

> "We are good friends to one another and offer support when someone needs a boost."
> –Judy Huitt

- Fabric
- Red headband
- Purple and red feathers
- Red silk rose
- Red boa
- Rhinestones

A Few of My Favorite Things

Queen Elegante

Earlene Holladay
R.E.D. B.U.D.S. (Refined
Exceptional Dames Being Utterly
Dedicated to Serendipity)
Columbia, California

"When I put on a red hat I come alive, joyful, and happy," says Earlene Holladay. "Everything I do is exciting and fun. I have no cares or worries and I feel good all over. I laugh more when I'm wearing my red hat."

Earlene sought out this hat while vacationing in Arizona one year.

Some months later Earlene stopped by a flower shop, where she happened upon a bushel of artificial cherries, berries, green leaves, and a silk flower, and the rest, they say, is Red Hat history.

Earlene secured her embellishments to the velvet hat with a hot glue gun and added a Queen lapel pin.

While Earlene is plenty outgoing and friendly, she says her red hat gives her license to be outrageous.

"My chapter walks in the Fourth of July parade in the historic Gold Rush town of Columbia," says Earlene. "We've won first place in our category [women over 50] four years in a row."

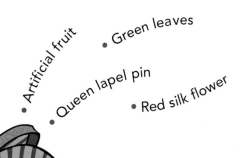

- Artificial fruit
- Green leaves
- Queen lapel pin
- Red silk flower

A Few of My Favorite Things

Countess Cool Cat

Pat Disher
Old Bats in Red Hats
Stoney Creek, Ontario, Canada

One day Pat Disher and her fellow chapterettes were approached by a local cable T.V. producer, who invited them to appear on her show. Wanting something unique to wear, Pat pulled out an old hat and got to work adding flower petals and silk flowers to her heart's content.

"I like to be different and stand out in a crowd, which goes hand-in-hand with my love of wearing unique, one-of-a-kind clothing and accessories," says Pat, who named herself the Countess Cool Cat "to rebel against the old in our chapter's name."

Her red hat is not just a fashion statement; it allows her to show her Red Hat Society spirit.

"Before I became a Red Hatter, I found it very difficult to accept the results of aging and hated those 'milestone' birthdays," says Pat. "Now, when I put on my red hat, I feel young at heart and forget about my wrinkles, extra pounds, and aches and pains and focus instead on the joy of another fun-filled get-together with my chapter sisters."

Hat How-To

Materials

- Fabric paint: purple
- Ribbon: purple
- Silk rose petals: red
- Silk roses: red
- Tulle: purple

Instructions

1. Paint edges of hat brim with purple fabric paint. Hot glue first circle of petals around outer edge of brim, overlapping previous petal. Continue with enough rows to cover brim.

2. For underside of brim, repeat steps for upper brim until underneath is covered with petals. Tuck petal bases of innermost circle into crown and glue to inner crown surface.

3. For crown, glue first circle of crown petals around outer edge of crown, making sure each petal overlaps previous petal and overlaps curve of crown. Continue with enough rows to cover crown. To cover gap in center of crown, glue small silk rose in center.

4. For hatband, measure circumference of crown and cut two lengths of 1½"-wide purple ribbon. Glue each length of ribbon around crown, overlapping edges slightly.

5. Pull roses off stems; arrange around brim of hat, close to crown, and hot glue in place. Tuck in a few green leaves pulled from stems and glue in place.

6. To create pouf bows, cut 1½ yards of 6"-wide purple tulle, then cut tulle into five equal pieces. Fold each piece in half and tie into a knot. You will now have a "pouf bow" with a single loop, a knot, and two tails. Tuck bows among roses and glue in place.

7. If desired, create large bow with 1½ yards of same purple tulle and position at back of hat; pin or hot glue it under brim.

Bloomin' Joan

Joan Ashton
KindRed Sisters
Fremont, California

Joan Ashton loves shopping for red hats—not just for the thrill of the find but also for the attention she receives.

"People say, 'Oh, you are with the Red Hat Society,' if you are shopping for a red hat," says Joan. "Otherwise people would walk right past you."

Joan found this particular vintage felt hat at a white elephant sale several years ago. It evolved into its splendor over time as Joan found pieces to add. Feathers, butterflies, and vintage roses were artfully arranged with a needle and thread.

"The hat speaks friendliness and peace," says Joan. "The Red Hat Society says that through the hats, it brings people together."

The KindRed Sisters enjoy connecting with the dynamic women of other local chapters. They often meet for tea, tours of historic houses, movies, and even "A Party to Dye For," in which they colored their clothing various shades of purple. Everything from underwear to slacks got a regal makeover.

- Bright neon red and purple feathers
- Fabric butterflies
- Rosy watermelon and rosy pink vintage fabric roses

A Few of My Favorite Things

Lady Patti Pan

Patricia Ann Crane
Disney Darlings
Northridge, California

Who says Disneyland is just for kids? Certainly not Patricia Ann Crane, who's proud to strut her red hot stuff at the theme park twice a month with her chapter.

"I love to act silly and make friends," says Patricia Ann. "With a red hat on my head I have found that there are a lot more people who also like to make friends and act silly."

Patricia Ann found her hat at a diner on a road trip to Las Vegas, and after several Red Hat Society chapter events she was ready to get crafty and decorate a hat of her own.

Patricia Ann gathered some buttons and a lighted puff she had bought at the Red Hat Society store and got to work. She dug into her collection of lapel pins and adorned her hat with Mary Poppins Practically Perfect Tea, Disney 50th Anniversary Tea, Golden Teacups, and a pin featuring a Mad Hatter and Cheshire cat balancing tea cups. It took two hours to perfectly place every pin, but the results, says Patricia Ann, were well worth it.

- Feather puff
- Purple marabou
- Flower buttons
- Silk roses
- Lapel pins
- Lighted puff

Favorite Things

Queen Diva

Susan Stopera
Spindle City Divas
Cohoes, New York

"It's amazing what a red hat can do; it starts up many conversations and compliments," says Susan Stopera.

This particular Victorian era-inspired hat is a favorite of her collection of 30-plus hats.

Recalling photographs of Victorian ladies in their lovely hats, Susan got to work on her own period design. First, she stripped a felt hat of all its decorations. She attached cotton batting around and on top of the crown to create a full look, and then covered the hat with embossed velvet, wiring the material tightly at the crown. The rest of the fabric was brought out to the brim, then tucked under the brim and pinned down. She then sewed down the fabric all the way around the hat by hand, through both the material and the hat. With a hot glue gun, she attached the lace around the brim, and then tied a strip of tulle around the crown. Around the base of the hat Susan glued feather trim and silk roses.

"Whether the hat is sassy, regal, or just simply funny," says Susan, "it's all in the hattitude."

- Cotton batting
- Red embossed velvet
- Feather trim
- Purple lace
- Purple tulle
- Red silk roses

A Few of My Favorite Things

Princess Starred & Feathered Darling Darla

Darla Taylor
Ruby Red Hatters Chapter 1
Tampa, Florida

A basic straw hat with a brim was all Darla Taylor needed to get her into a Red Hat Society hat party.

"I first decided what style of hat I liked then went to the local crafts store and picked up some paint," says Princess Starred & Feathered Darling Darla. "The rest I just dreamed up."

After she spray painted the hat several times, Darla made a hatband by wrapping the brim with ribbon, securing it in place at the back with hot glue. She then took one side of the brim and folded it up, securing it carefully with hot glue. A ribbon bow was made for the back, which was glued in several places and positioned onto the hat. Finishing embellishments include silk flowers with their stems clipped off and star embellishments hot glued onto the hat.

Says Darla, "And there you have it—your own stylish, fancy hat to go to lunch with the girls—original hattitude!"

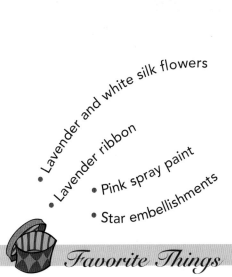

- Lavender and white silk flowers
- Lavender ribbon
- Pink spray paint
- Star embellishments

Favorite Things

Queen Bee

Ella Whitaker
L.O.V.E. Red Hats
Middleburg, Florida

It was a chapter affair when Ella Whitaker decided to create this tuity-fruity hat.

At a craft party for her chapter, Ella pulled out a Mexican sombrero and spray painted it red. Some helped in gluing on items while others gave her pointers on where to place the plastic bananas, cherries, watermelon, apples, oranges, bunches of grapes, lemons, pears, and plums.

But before she picked and placed the fruit, Ella covered the crown of the hat with purple tulle, hot glued in place at the base of the hat. She then added silk flowers and fruit and a purple garland around the brim of the hat. The finishing touch is the green parrot perched at top.

"My Carmen Miranda hat says that I am a woman that has a lot of carefree spirit," says Ella.

The hat also says she's a winner.

"I won a first place prize at the second annual Palatka, Florida Red Hat Festival in 2004," says Ella, "during the weekend of Hurricane Ivan!"

- Plastic fruit
- Purple tulle
- Red spray paint
- Purple garland
- Toy parrot
- Purple iris and red rose silk flowers

A Few of My Favorite Things

Chapter 7

Simple Hats & Sporty Caps

Red Hatters are as sporty as the next gals, right? We may not paint our chests green and white, but you can be sure our favorite sports team will be seeing red when they look up into the stands and are dazzled by our various visors filled with vibrant detail.

Whether your very extraordinary visor accompanies you to the next Red Sox game or you're flaunting it while walking with your favorite girlfriends, make sure you give it everything you've got. The mantra for us hat-happy folk is that a hat worth wearing is a hat worth decorating. So while a visor might be something an ordinary person grabs at the last minute when the sun's out, your impeccably attired visor will shine like a beacon, causing all eyes to be on you.

We've known some sporting events where the fantastic hats have completely eclipsed what was happening on the field. This does not make that $6 million-a-year first baseman very happy but it sure has made sporty hats into a very popular pastime. Next thing you know, you can sell your own tickets and make a fortune. Don't forget the rest of your Red Hat Society sisters when you do!

"We just know inside that we're queens. And these are the crowns we wear." —Felecia McMillan

Sweet Eleanore

Eleanore Matheson
Crazy Daisies
Santa Ana, California

Eleanore Matheson is living up to her chapter's name—and everything's coming up daisies.

"My red hat was designed and created by someone with a very fun-loving personality—me," says Red Hatter Sweet Eleanore. "I love the attention it gets because it is so silly."

To create this garden delight, Eleanore simply hot glued the daisies to the hat, adding safety pins here and there for extra support. She had borrowed the hat some time ago and it seems the hat is staying put on this Red Hatter's head.

"Our Queen Mother, Maggie Pohlman, lent me the hat when I participated in my first Red Hat Society activity and did not have a red hat," says Eleanore. "Obviously now she will never get it back!"

My friends think I'm nutty in a nice way
For years I've heard that said
But just to prove them wrong
I now wear purple and red.

Who could not admire the flair
They'll now know I am not crazy
When I mix purple and red
And top it off with a daisy!

–Eleanore Matheson

- Red baseball cap
- Silk daisies

Favorite Things

114

Mz. P.A. Proper

Jennifer Taormina-Smiley
Hens & Chicks
Reno, Nevada

When Jennifer Smiley was a girl, her mother diligently put her to bed early.

Today, Jennifer and her mom, both members of the Red Hat Society, stay up all night long sewing, cutting, and gluing embellishments to pink and red hats to wear to chapter gatherings.

Jennifer picked up the lavender foam visor at a discount store and looked through a box of her wedding memorabilia for inspiration.

"For my pink visor I chose pretentious pearls, lace for mystery, and tassels for fun," says Jennifer.

The pearl spray and satin ribbon are from wedding corsages and the small flowers are off favors from her bridal shower. Lavender lace and tassel trim were adhered onto the rim of the hat with a hot glue gun.

"Lavender is one of my favorite colors—I used it in my wedding and now I wear it today," says Jennifer.

"We are all mothers and daughters. We started our chapter so that we would all get together and have fun without husbands or kids. With just the girls we can really be ourselves." –Jennifer Taormina-Smiley

- Lavender lace
- Lavender satin ribbon
- Lavender tassel trim
- Feathers
- Pearl spray
- Lavender silk flowers
- String of pearls

A Few of My Favorite Things

Princess Norma Jean of Cypress

Norma Jean Lipert
Red Hot Mommas with Hattitudes
Cypress, Texas
Hat modeled by Jayne Cosh

"When I wear my red hat, away goes my tension; I become funny and silly, the center of attention," enthuses Norma Jean Lipert.

This Red Hatter wanted something casual for outdoor activities, yet fun-loving and spirited. After she found this red visor at a craft store, Norma Jean started on her hunt for the perfect embellishments, designing the hat as she went along. She added red and purple ribbon, which she tied into bows, to the side of the hat, then filled in the rest of the visor with purple foam shapes. Silver glitter, applied in swirls, adds sparkle and the purple feather tops off the hat with Red Hat Society sass.

"My hat says, 'Look at me,'" says Norma Jean. "I am flashy and silly and playful. But most of all, I am young at heart."

- Purple and red ribbons
- Silver glitter paint
- Purple feather
- Purple foam cutouts

A Few of My Favorite Things

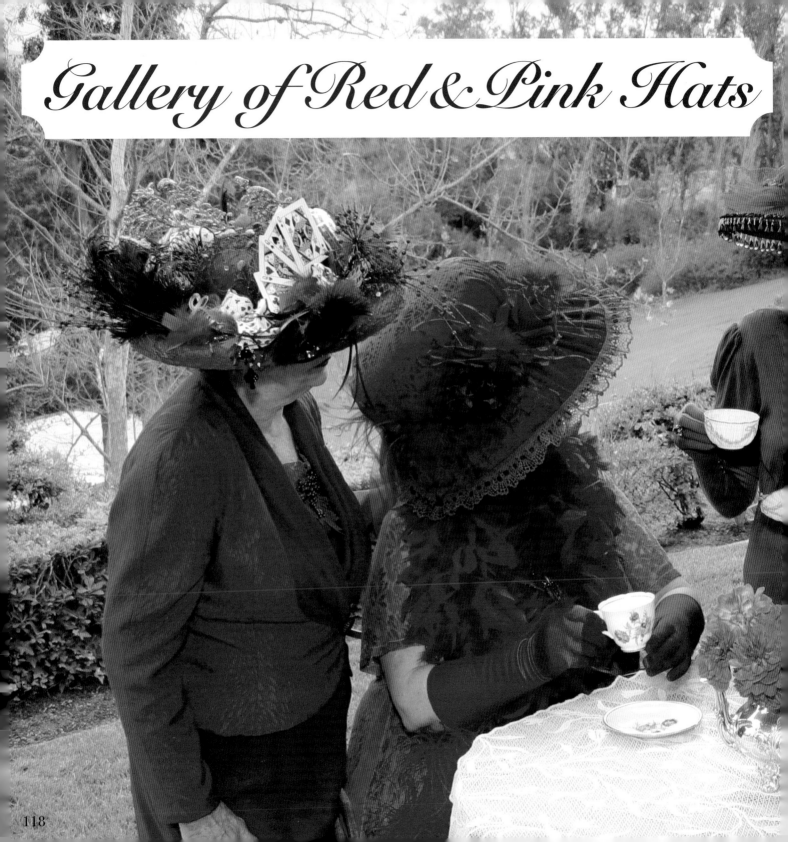

Gallery of Red & Pink Hats

Ann Nickerson
Serendipity Sisters
Snohomish, Washington

"This Mad Hatter hat started out as a Dr. Seuss hat. It was made of red velvet so I cut it down and sewed it back together then added sequins, a ribbon band, tulle, and two purple roses for style and chic."

Lois Elliott
Bodacious Babes
Phoenix, Arizona

"My hat says I am outgoing and a person who has fun. Because of my warm personality people are attracted to me and I grab them into my 'web' of fun."

Carlotta Wixon
Sierra Sirens
Grass Valley, California

"I bought this red straw hat years ago, long before I knew there would ever be a Red Hat Society. I draped satin over the hat then added poinsettias, ribbon, and my crowning glory, a Queen rhinestone pin—it's one of 14 rhinestone crowns I have!"

Jackie Singmaster
Annapolis Red Hat Ladies
Annapolis, Maryland

"I decided to make a hat so I could display the beautiful rooster feather. Donning a red hat brings out the independent and more 'fun-loving' me."

Cynthia Feagle
Bodacious Red Hats
of San Diego
San Diego, California

"I just keep adding
and adding to it," says
Cynthia, who belongs
to a chapter of mostly
quilters. "It gets heavier
and heavier."

Karin Christie
The Rockettes of Eagle Rock
Los Angeles, California

"Along with everyone else in the
Rockettes, I fell in love with the
red hat that Carolyn Sawyer,
my chapter sister, had made for
herself. I was so touched when
she offered her talents to work
with me to create a pink one.
It turned out just as I wanted
and each time I wear it I feel
like a very special Pink Hatter!"

Barbara Donaldson
The El Monte Yacht Club
El Monte, California

"It means so much to my sister to wear
hats, and red ones are even better,"
says Barbara, who cares for her sister
and fellow chapterette, Sandy, a terminal cancer patient. "She has 30 hats and
because of her I'm a Red Hatter. I'm
even decorating hats alongside her."

Carol Orbeck
Bling Bats in Red Hats
Gold River, California

"My hat says I'm
having fun and I get
to share that with
anyone who notices
the hat. As always,
it's all about the hat!"

Ella Whitaker
L.O.V.E. Red Hats
Middleburg, Florida

"Our chapter didn't do anything for Halloween one year and several of us wanted to go to our monthly luncheon dressed up in some type of costume. And of course we just had to use the red hat witch idea."

Beverly Taormina
Hens & Chicks
Reno, Nevada

"Most of my hats have detachable pieces that can be put on other hats. I look at the shape of the hat and go for it!"

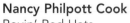

Nancy Philpott Cook
Rovin' Red Hats
Winchester, Massachussetts

"Having a red hat proudly perched on my head confirms that I am sharing fun and friendship with my contemporaries around the globe. Wearing my hat causes others around me to smile, thus warming my own heart."

Carol Bobo
Heavenly Hatters
Santa Cruz, California

"I have approximately 40 hats and since I now have 'scarlet fever,' I only see red and purple when I am shopping. I'm always on the lookout for hats. I do not wear the same hat decorated the same way twice, therefore I attach the adornments in a way that they can be removed and changed."

Credits

A Red Lips 4 Courage book
Red Lips 4 Courage Communications, Inc.:
Eileen Cannon Paulin, Catherine Risling,
Rebecca Ittner, Jayne Cosh
8502 E. Chapman Ave., 303
Orange, CA 92869

Book Editor:
Catherine Risling

Contributing Writers:
Erika Kotite
Catherine Risling

Photo Stylist:
Rebecca Ittner

Book Designer:
Kehoe + Kehoe Design Associates, Inc.
Burlington, Vermont

Photographer:
Denny Nelson

Acknowledgments

Thank you to our Red Hatters who served as models
for hats from all over the country: Margaret
Manchester Brown, Kay Foster, Carol Ritter,
Marylou Rogers, and Joan Taylor of the Beaded Babes,
Fullerton, CA; Eleanore Matheson and Maggie
Pohlman of The Crazy Daisies, Tustin/Santa Ana, CA;
and Polly Laughlin of The Founding Chapter,
Fullerton, CA.

METRIC EQUIVALENCY CHARTS

inches to millimeters (mm) and centimeters (cm)

inches	mm	cm	inches	cm	inches	cm
1/8	3	0.3	9	22.9	30	76.2
1/4	6	0.6	10	25.4	31	78.7
1/2	13	1.3	12	30.5	33	83.8
5/8	16	1.6	13	33.0	34	86.4
3/4	19	1.9	14	35.6	35	88.9
7/8	22	2.2	15	38.1	36	91.4
1	25	2.5	16	40.6	37	94.0
1¼	32	3.2	17	43.2	38	96.5
1½	38	3.8	18	45.7	39	99.1
1¾	44	4.4	19	48.3	40	101.6
2	51	5.1	20	50.8	41	104.1
2½	64	6.4	21	53.3	42	106.7
3	76	7.6	22	55.9	43	109.2
3½	89	8.9	23	58.4	44	111.8
4	102	10.2	24	61.0	45	114.3
4½	114	11.4	25	63.5	46	116.8
5	127	12.7	26	66.0	47	119.4
6	152	15.2	27	68.6	48	121.9
7	178	17.8	28	71.1	49	124.5
8	203	20.3	29	73.7	50	127.0

yards to meters

yards	meters	yards	meters	yards	meters	yards	meters	yards	meters
1/8	0.11	2⅛	1.94	4⅛	3.77	6⅛	5.60	8⅛	7.43
1/4	0.23	2¼	2.06	4¼	3.89	6¼	5.72	8¼	7.54
3/8	0.34	2⅜	2.17	4⅜	4.00	6⅜	5.83	8⅜	7.66
1/2	0.46	2½	2.29	4½	4.11	6½	5.94	8½	7.77
5/8	0.57	2⅝	2.40	4⅝	4.23	6⅝	6.06	8⅝	7.89
3/4	0.69	2¾	2.51	4¾	4.34	6¾	6.17	8¾	8.00
7/8	0.80	2⅞	2.63	4⅞	4.46	6⅞	6.29	8⅞	8.12
1	0.91	3	2.74	5	4.57	7	6.40	9	8.23
1⅛	1.03	3⅛	2.86	5⅛	4.69	7⅛	6.52	9⅛	8.34
1¼	1.14	3¼	2.97	5¼	4.80	7¼	6.63	9¼	8.46
1⅜	1.26	3⅜	3.09	5⅜	4.91	7⅜	6.74	9⅜	8.57
1½	1.37	3½	3.20	5½	5.03	7½	6.86	9½	8.69
1⅝	1.49	3⅝	3.31	5⅝	5.14	7⅝	6.97	9⅝	8.80
1¾	1.60	3¾	3.43	5¾	5.26	7¾	7.09	9¾	8.92
1⅞	1.71	3⅞	3.54	5⅞	5.37	7⅞	7.20	9⅞	9.03
2	1.83	4	3.66	6	5.49	8	7.32	10	9.14

Index

So much more than purple

and red.

The Red Hat Society® is an international "disorganization" of women who embrace the worth of deepening friendships and rediscovering the value of play.

Underneath the frivolity, we share a bond of affection and a genuine enthusiasm for wherever life takes us next.

To learn more about the Red Hat Society, please visit **www.redhatsociety.com**

To request membership information by mail, please send your name, address and phone number to: Red Hat Society Information Requests, P.O. Box 768, Fullerton, CA 92836.

There's Only One... Join The Fun!